PENNSYLVANIA FIRESIDE TALES

VOLUME 5

JEFFREY R. FRAZIER

CATAMOUNT
PRESS

an imprint of Sunbury Press, Inc.
Mechanicsburg, PA USA

CATAMOUNT
PRESS

an imprint of Sunbury Press, Inc.
Mechanicsburg, PA USA

For information about special discounts for bulk purchases, please contact Sunbury Press Orders Dept. at (855) 338-8359 or orders@sunburypress.com.

To request one of our authors for speaking engagements or book signings, please contact Sunbury Press Publicity Dept. at publicity@sunburypress.com.

FIRST CATAMOUNT PRESS EDITION: October 2024

Set in Adobe Garamond | Interior design by Crystal Devine | Cover by Lawrence Knorr | Edited by Debra Reynolds.

Publisher's Cataloging-in-Publication Data
Names: Frazier, Jeffrey R., author.
Title: Pennsylvania fireside tales volume 5 / Jeffrey R. Frazier.
Description: First trade paperback edition. | Mechanicsburg, PA : Catamount Press, 2024.
Summary: Volume 5 in the Pennsylvania Fireside Tales series exploring the origins and foundations of old-time Pennsylvania mountain folktales, legends, and folklore.
Identifiers: ISBN : 979-8-88819-231-3 (paperback).
Subjects: NATURE / Ecosystems & Habitats / Mountains | HISTORY / United States / State & Local / Middle Atlantic (DC, DE, MD, NJ, NY, PA) | FICTION / Fairy Tales, Folk Tales & Mythology.

Designed in the USA
0 1 1 2 3 5 8 13 21 34 55

For the Love of Books!

Cover: Based on Alexander Carse (British, circa 1770–1843) Tavern scene oil on canvas 44.5 x 60cm (17 1/2 x 23 5/8in).

To my parents and both my grandmothers,
from whom I learned to love Pennsylvania's mountains,
and to the old-time mountain folks whose stories
form the soul of these awe-inspiring hills.

The Old Hitchin' Post. Here, decades ago, visitors' horses were tethered while their owners paid a visit to the owners of Elmwood Farms in Mackeyville, Clinton County. See the chapter titled "A Trophy Buck" in the author's Pennsylvania Fireside Tales Volume IV *for some old-time tales from the forests surrounding this picturesque homestead.*

CONTENTS

— ALSO BY —
JEFFREY R. FRAZIER

Pennsylvania Fireside Tales Volume I

The Black Ghost of Scotia & More Pennsylvania Fireside Tales Volume II

Pennsylvania Fireside Tales Volumes III–VIII

Pennsylvania Fireside Ghost Tales

Pennsylvania Mountain Landmarks Volumes I–III

It's always seemed to me that legends and yarns and folktales are as much a part of the real history of a country as proclamations and provisos and constitutional amendments.

—Rudyard Kipling

INTRODUCTION

Although four other volumes of Pennsylvania folktales and legends have already been presented to the public by this writer, I feel that my task is not complete until I've published all the tales I've collected over the last thirty years that seem worthy of preservation for the enjoyment of future generations. If nothing else, these old stories, some of whose roots may span back to the dawn of storytelling itself, show how little some of humankinds' basic thoughts and desires have changed over the centuries, and conversely, how far we've come in discarding the yoke of ignorance and superstition that held back our ancient ancestors. Taken together, these human foibles, and the qualities that offset them, produced the many enjoyable anecdotes that now form the fabric of Pennsylvania's oral history and legendary lore.

It is this human-interest side of the stories that I like to explore and emphasize in my books, and which never seems to get emphasized enough when the tales are normally presented to the public by folklorists and by the entertainment industry. Likewise, these dispensers of such material don't seem to make a whole lot of effort to explain to the general public where the tales came from in the first place, and that's the other thing I like to explore in my books.

I've always felt that there's something mystical about the Pennsylvania mountains, and that's probably why I've always had the same opinion about their folktales and legends. The state's mountains have never ceased to stir my sense of wonder, and the old tales that cluster around them hold the same allure. For me these mountains have always been a place of superstition and romance, and no other experiences in my life have been as uplifting as the hikes and drives through some of the most picturesque mountainous regions of the state.

Among those trips were those taken in search of Pennsylvania's grandest panoramas and its most mysterious places. One such excursion was a visit to the Pinnacle in Berks County, where a majestic view of Berks, Lehigh, and Schuylkill Counties was the reward for completing the steep hike up to one of the state's most unusual rock formations. Similarly etched into my mind are the many hikes taken into the Blue Mountains of Dauphin County for a visit to the mysterious King's Stool above Clarks Valley, and up into the South Mountains of Adams and Franklin Counties in search of the elusive Indian face. Last but not least were jaunts into the mysterious Black Forest regions of Potter, Elk, and Tioga Counties, as well as grand excursions into the Bald Eagles of Lycoming and Clinton Counties.

Of course, the Seven Mountains of Centre and Mifflin Counties have always held a special appeal for me. They were a treasure trove of the old traditions when I started collecting such tales over thirty years ago, and I'm always reminded of that fact when I pass through this glorious region, which, I'm sure, will always be a source of solace and peace for me.

Although I've been mining Pennsylvania's lode of legends and folktales for over fifty years, and writing about them for over thirty years, I look back upon the endeavor with pleasure as well as regret. It's nice to know that I've preserved the tales, even though I've neither done so using the strict scientific process that scholars of such things would use, nor in a format that would meet the standards required by those formally trained in the disciplines of history, folklore, philology, and the other related sciences, that a disciplined study of such tales really requires. Nonetheless, for me it's enough to know that no matter how imperfectly the task has been done, I've done the best I can, and the tales have been researched in a way that has satisfied my own curiosity.

That's not to say that I'm completely satisfied. There's always that feeling that no matter how much you've done or how far you've gone, you still don't have the complete picture as to the origins of a tale that oftentimes sounds like what today we'd call far-fetched. After all, you can only take these things back so far, and then you begin to realize that you've hit a stone wall. The question repeatedly arises, how many stories, or details about them, lie slumbering in the grave with the one who would have willingly passed them on to anyone who had taken the time to listen?

I've mentioned many examples of stories like this that I've collected and then written about in previous volumes; and in the present volume, the story of the Headless Ghost of Penn's Creek is one more. Here the tale claims that the decapitated spirit that haunts a lonely stretch of road near the village of Spring Mills in Centre County is that of a railroad switchman. However, based on old topographic maps, it doesn't appear that a switchman would have been needed where his unfortunate accident supposedly occurred.

In this isolated section of the mountains, there appear to have been no other tracks that a switchman would have been able to switch a train onto at all! Nonetheless, despite the apparent contradictions, the apparition still manifests itself to late night travelers from time to time, its most recent appearance being within the last two years.

It's just another example of how confusing and maddeningly frustrating legends and folktales can be, when anyone tries to explore their origins and investigate their details. It would be nice to have the time to thoroughly check such details out, but until I retire, it's just not possible. Perhaps someday, but for now I have to be content to pursue the same course I have followed thus far.

To me, a good writer is like a good artist. Both should note minute details that the average person does not see, and then include them in the final product they produce. That's what I've tried to do in the stories I've preserved, in this and in previous volumes; and based on responses from public and press alike, the approach seems to have been accepted and the results even somewhat enjoyable. I'm gratified by that, and I'm looking forward to writing Volume VI as a result of this support.

Once again, I'd like to thank my son for his artwork in this volume, and also would like to thank all those who continue to call and write with words of appreciation and encouragement. Contacts like this led me to still more stories and storytellers, and I appreciate the help. I thought that the treasure lode of such material would have been exhausted by now, but the old tales continue to survive, just as they have managed to do for uncounted centuries, and perhaps just as they will continue to do for many more centuries to come.

AUTHOR'S NOTE

The preceding paragraphs are what appeared in the first and second editions of this volume, and this new Sunbury Press paperback edition contains the same chapters and photos that appeared in the last hardback edition of this same work. However, at the request of the publisher, I have added new material, including interesting details that were discovered when doing research for this edition. This edition also includes new photos and better-quality versions of the original photos. I think these improvements, as in previous editions, will add a whole new level of interest to the original tales. I hope these enhancements add to the reader's enjoyment.

CHAPTER 1

MOUNTAIN LANDMARKS

Mountains, when viewed from a distance, can seem like lonely and mysterious places, almost uninviting in their dark and cheerless demeanor. On the other hand, despite their somber aspects, the old ridges still appeal to lovers of the outdoors and to the curious who like to ponder about the silent marvels that might lie hidden beneath the forest canopy that covers the mountain slopes. Although such thoughts might sound like pipe dreams to some, it is a fact that these time-worn peaks sometimes do conceal unusual and mysterious formations and landmarks in their rocky glens and deep woods; appealing mysteries that are almost as ancient as the hills themselves; marvels wrapped in centuries-old enigmas that seem to be unsolvable.

Counted among these kinds of places are the impressive natural formations that cause onlookers to pause and take a second look; the scenic wonders that hikers, hunters, and casual weekend sightseers might find as they traverse the back roads, deep valleys, and winding trails of Pennsylvania's mountains. Some would say that prominent among these landmarks is the unusual Dinosaur Rock in the foothills of Lebanon County. There are many others that might be mentioned as well, including the rock city of gigantic sandstone boulders known as Bilger's Rocks over in Clearfield County. Pulpit Rock on Warriors Ridge in Blair County is yet another place worthy of mention, not only because of its unusual title but also due to its supposed connection with the many Indians who once called Warriors Ridge their hunting ground.

As the name suggests, Pulpit Rock does resemble a gigantic lectern, and as such brings to mind a huge altar used in ancient times by a mysterious Druid-like people. Although Druidic fires never burned here, it is said that it may have indeed been a place where the smoke from Indian council fires could once be seen. Indeed, the notion that Indians were somehow connected to such spots is a common one, and this idea becomes even more appealing to one who finds stone constructs or earthen mounds that were obviously fashioned by the hands of man sometime in the distant past, but which somehow seem out of place today.

Stone walls or large earthen mounds, on an isolated mountaintop or down in the depths of some dark and forbidding hollow, have an aura of mystery about them; a sense that they are products of an age that preceded even that of the first colonists who settled here. In such cases, the tendency to think that Indians were the builders of such things is a natural one. Nonetheless, such judgments are often premature, arising from lack of more plausible explanations, and bolstered by the fact that Native Americans did often leave evidence of their existence, on the rocks, and in the names of the valleys, mountains, and streams which they once called their own.

The unique signatures of Pennsylvania's Native Americans were certainly familiar to the early settlers of Pennsylvania who found them in the form of rock engravings or carvings and pictures on trees. These same settlers also found a vast system of trails that had been used for countless years prior to entry of any colonials, and along these paths were the warrior's marks—carvings and pictures on trees or on rocks which proved that the natives used the path.

Sometimes, too, there would be an Indian bridge, which allowed a traveler to cross a rushing stream without getting his feet wet. Such bridges were just tall trees, which had been toppled so that they spanned the waters of the creek. Once the branches of the fallen forest monarch were trimmed away, the remaining log was an effective foot bridge, and yet another landmark that linked the Indian to the land on which he lived.

Landmarks such as native bridges and tree markings were only but fleeting reminders of the aboriginal culture which was here before the colonists came to settle the same lands, and about the only new evidence of the original people that the average person uncovers anymore are the black flint arrowheads that surface in a farmer's field now and then. Those who have made it their hobby to find these souvenirs know that fields aren't the only places to find them; the west side of streams proving to be fruitful ground as well.

The reason for looking there, they say, is that since prevailing winds are from west to east, a warrior would always try to get downwind from the animals he was hunting with his bow and arrow. Since the game he was stalking would frequently be along a stream, an Indian would often be shooting at animals over on the west bank. However, even the seekers who know such secrets for finding arrowheads admit that the number that can be found gets less and less every year, and perhaps it is for this reason that we grasp for other reminders of the Indian, no matter how unlikely it may be that they have any connection with him at all.

There are a number of unusual mountain landmarks that people have decided are of native origin, when in fact, there is little or no evidence to substantiate those claims, but one notable exception to such places may be the numerous earthen mounds that lie on top of a small hillock in Georges Valley, Centre County. Some older residents of the valley still say that the mounds are graves of Indians; but scholars don't seem to feel the same way and have not been inclined to conduct any excavations to settle the matter one way or another. Years ago, a curious valley resident dug into one of the mounds but found no bones or relics of any kind. What he did find was something that appeared to be a quantity of ochre, the orange pigment sometimes used by the natives for funereal and other ceremonial purposes.

Despite the lack of convincing tangible evidence regarding the exact nature of the Georges Valley mounds, the folktales of the region are definite about the matter, recalling that the first valley settlers were told by the area's remaining Indians that a large battle between warring tribes once took place here. Twenty years ago, there were still valley residents who remembered this tradition, as well as yet another.

This second piece of oral history preserves the idea that there was once a native village in the fields beside the creek that courses along the foot of the little ridge on which the mounds are located. Some valley residents, spurred on by both legends, have searched for and found many arrowheads in and around the fields where the village once stood and where the great fight supposedly occurred, but other than those bits of scanty evidence, no historical accounts exist which preserve a record of a battle anywhere in this valley.

There is one historical account that does provide some confirmation for part of the legend, however; and that is a record of a skirmish between colonists and natives that took place near Duboistown, Lycoming County, in 1779. The description of how the warriors buried their dead compatriots after that fight is based on a deposition from Moses Van Campen, one of the most determined Indian fighters of the entire West Branch Valley. Taken prisoner at this particular battle, Van Campen noticed that the victors wasted no time in burying their fallen comrades.

According to the old borderer's first-hand account, the exercise was a simple one. First, they merely rolled an old log away from its resting place. Then, to complete the burials, they laid the bodies in the exposed hollow and "heaped upon them a little earth."[1]

Historical evidence verifying legendary claims of native origins is typically hard to find for places like the Georges Valley mounds, and when such evidence does surface it's got to be indisputable to convince the skeptics, mainly because such legends have often been proven to be untrue. In some cases, it's apparent that nature alone was responsible for creating the structures and shapes that form distinctive landmarks found in isolated spots in the mountains. In other instances, it's just as apparent that the hand of man was at work, and in these cases, it's often the gray area of legends and folktales that's relied upon for clues as to the builders.

One of the more unusual spots that could be placed in this category is a Stonehenge-like formation once said to lie in a field in northern Centre County, where many large upright stones stand as silent sentinels, much like the famous Easter Island figures of the eastern Pacific. Although apparently set up for some ceremonial purpose, no one today has any idea as to who might have arranged the Centre County stones in this way or for exactly what reason. Some theorize that they may even be the remaining parts of a fortress of some sort, but there is no evidence to support this idea either.

---

1. John Blair Linn, *History of Centre and Clinton Counties*, 652.

Even legends seem silent about the matter, and so it would seem that the men who placed the stones in this way and why they did so will always remain a mystery, especially now that this mysterious place can no longer be found.

With the exception of the standing stone that was the totem for the tribe who lived on the site of what is now Huntingdon in Huntingdon County, there is no evidence that Pennsylvania Indians stood rocks up like this, in Centre County or in any other place in the state either. Likewise, there is no evidence to connect the Centre County site with the builders who constructed the many rock walls and accompanying stone piles found on Nittany Mountain of Centre County (which, along with similar sites all along the east coast, have baffled scholars for centuries—see the story entitled "Council Rocks" in the author's Pennsylvania Fireside Tales, Volume IV, for details on the theories as to the origins of the walls and the legend that still clings to this spot).

Mysterious spots like the standing stones in Centre County, or the rock walls on Nittany Mountain of Centre County, capture our imaginations and draw us to them, but they are certainly not the only remarkable places like that in Pennsylvania. There is yet another unusual landmark in the central Pennsylvania mountains that has kept its secrets as well as the sites of the standing stones and Council Rocks in Centre County, and that is the place of the stone steps on Tussey Mountain near the village of Pine Grove Mills, Centre County.

The Indian Steps, as the stone stairway on Tussey Mountain is called, have baffled people for decades. Extending all the way down the south face of the mountain, the steps are known to have existed as early as at least 1900, but references to them prior to that time surface only in legendary accounts, and so the builders of the steps are just as much a mystery today as they were a hundred years ago. The most popular account of their origin, and which no doubt is the basis for the name, is that the natives of Stone Valley built them to use in a surprise attack on the warriors in the valleys to the north.

Based on what is known about early Indian warfare tactics, there is little likelihood that one tribe would have gone to the trouble of building the Indian Steps in hopes of using them to surprise their enemy in a lightning

View of the Indian Steps. Tussey Mountain, Centre and Huntingdon Counties.

attack. The effort required to build the steps would have resulted in a flurry of activity, which certainly would have been noticed by hunters and scouts of the enemy tribe.

Nor is it likely that any natives would believe in the first place that they could undertake such a project without being detected. One of the most basic tactics used in Indian warfare was the element of surprise. Building stone steps up one side of a mountain to use in a surprise attack on an enemy tribe right on the other side of the same mountain would not

The author standing at the foot of the Indian Steps in Harry's Valley, Tussey Mountain, Huntingdon County.

have been a strategy employed by them. This tale of tribal warfare at the Indian Steps was first published and promoted by "fakelorist" Henry W. Shoemaker, and it has just recently been shown to be purely a Shoemaker fabrication.[2]

Other people have suggested that the Tussey Mountain steps were part of a trail that natives regularly used to cross Tussey Mountain; but the Standing Stone Path, just three miles away and an easier route, accomplished the

2. Simon J. Bronner, *Popularizing Pennsylvania*, 114.

same purpose. In fact, they would have had to make a detour off their normal routes to use the Indian Steps at all; and authorities like Paul Wallace, in his *Historic Indian Paths of Pennsylvania*, make no mention of the Steps, nor of any trails that might have been close enough to use them.

This lack of evidence about the origins of the Indian Steps on Tussey Mountain only heightens the aura of mystery that surrounds them and makes them seem unique. There is supposedly another flight of similar steps on the mountain near Livonia, Centre County, but I've never tried to verify whether they exist or not. If such stairs do exist, then the Livonia steps are yet another puzzle awaiting a detective to solve the mystery of their origins. Any such sleuth, it would seem, would soon determine that the best approach to discover the builders of any such unusual sites, including the Tussey Mountain steps, would be to identify similar landmarks and try to discover who built them.

In this writer's opinion, there are three such places that help to shed some light on the origins of the Indian Steps—an interesting path near Sterretts Gap on the Blue Mountain that divides the counties of Perry and Cumberland; impressive stone towers and a stone "fortress" that are discovered periodically by hunters and hikers on Nittany Mountain above Centre Hall, Centre County; and another stone stairway on the Blue Mountains north of Bethel in Berks County.

Hikers crossing the Blue Mountain due west of that scenic mountain passage named Sterretts Gap sometimes stumble upon a path outlined with stone borders on both sides, which extends up one side of the mountain and down the other. Although the name of the trail is probably now known only to a few old-time locals in the nearby villages of Shermans Dale or Dromgold, the path was still a prominent feature of the landscape up until twenty years ago, easily seen with a pair of binoculars from Route 944. It was along this same route that the story of Fox's Path was related to me one chilly afternoon in mid-February, when the leaves had long since fallen off the trees and the winds of winter swept over the Blue Mountain, chilling the landscape with their icy blasts.

"There was a guy by the name of Fox who lived over in Perry County, I guess he was just a farmer or trapper, and he would travel back and forth to Carlisle," explained the Cumberland County native whose ancestors were among the first settlers in the valley where he still lives today.

J. Ernest Wagner standing at his beloved "fort" on Nittany Mountain. (Photo taken by the author in 1988.)

"Of course that was back in the early days too," continued our informant. "In fact, this hollow over on the other side here is called Fox Hollow. Now when you had a gap or hollow named after you, you had to be the first one there. Where he'd be walking, he'd just take the stones and throw them off to the sides there, and you have a pile of stones that just goes up over the mountain.

"You can follow his trail over the mountain on both sides; it's just like a gully down through there. And on top of the mountain, he piled rocks up and made like a monument. It's laid up nice and square just like as if somebody took their time to face the stones and stuff and lay them up. I'd say it's probably about fifteen feet high, something like that. I imagine he crossed the mountain quite a few times because there's a pretty good gully down over the hill there where he picked the stones out."[3]

The extensive stone formations one person can build if he has the time, energy, and interest is indeed amazing, and another good example of one man's construction efforts are the stone towers and the stone fort found on Nittany Mountain above the village of Centre Hall in Centre County.

---

3. Ray Waggoner (born September 1, 1926), recorded February 17, 1980.

Known locally as Bennie's Fort and Bennie's Towers, these stone structures, some of which stand fifteen to twenty feet high, seem to be too massive to be the work of one man, but it actually took only one determined person to erect them some sixty years ago.

Known to his friends as "Ben," a nickname he acquired when he was a boy, J. Ernest Wagner of Centre Hall, was, at the time of our interview well "up into his nineties," as they say in the mountains. Still quite mentally alert, he happily claimed the honor of being the architect and builder of the Nittany Mountain stone monument. He did so, he explained, as a way of getting some exercise during the late 1930s and early 1940s. The whole project began when he was head of the Boy Scout troop in town, and he wanted an adventure to keep his scouts entertained.

The scoutmaster and his scouts would often engage in the usual activities enjoyed by hearty young fellows, playing games like touch football or baseball, but many times the allure of the nearby forest would pull them away from these more mundane pastimes and draw them to old Mount Nittany. Eventually, after mutually agreeing on a good spot, the scout troop laid out a trail from the mountain's first bench all the way to the top, and then, that grand project completed, began to pile up stones here and there just to have some fun.

Long after the scouts had become men, Ben continued the work on his own. Sunday afternoons were usually his favorite time, and once in a while he'd take someone along with him for help, including Harvey Flink, his cousin and the town's national award-winning poet. The result, over the years, are the towers that still stand today, and which are built from stones so huge in some cases that one has to wonder how one, or even two men, could have moved them into place.

"The big rocks I moved with a pry pole of dead chestnut," explained the old man one day when he escorted me up to his fort. "I had a pry pole maybe two and a half inches wide and maybe four and a half feet long, but quite a few of them I carried up the side or slid them down the mountain—down from up above. I just carried some there and when I got further up I'd tuck one under my arm and use my other hand, you know, to work my way up, and pile them up. I was rather good getting around that way, but I might've banged an ankle or bruised myself, and so on.

"Two or three years ago I was up on the mountain and coming down I just realized what could happen. I stepped between a couple rocks and over balanced, and I went down. It just happened I was going the way my knee bent. You could break a leg that way, getting your foot caught in a crevice and then falling. So, it ended up I didn't hurt myself. I never saw any snakes up there. In fact, from early on I seldom ever saw snakes when I was out hiking.

"I don't know. I think stones always fascinated me and I used to see some of these towers. For instance, what was the story of the boy who was held in the tower? Can't think of the title of it, but things like that fascinated me. Of course, my wife thought my time would have been better spent building us a house!"[4]

Spouses or relatives of the men who built Showers Steps in Berks County may have had sentiments similar to Ernest Wagner's wife, when they realized how much time Lloyd Showers and his brother were spending to build what they intended to be an access path to the Appalachian Trail on the Blue Mountain above Bethel. It's not known today if Lloyd or his brother were single or not during this period, but during the 1930s the two men devoted much of their free time in constructing their impressive stone stairway, which is still a favorite weekend climb for local hiking clubs.

Although it's enjoyable to see such spots firsthand, visits to these places are even more satisfying when the stories of their origins are not cloaked in mystery. It was, therefore, a pleasure for me to hear and preserve for posterity how Showers Steps and Fox's Path had been built and who had done so. And it was a greater pleasure to be able to meet the man who had built the Nittany Mountain towers, and an even greater thrill to be able to record the story of just how he managed to do it. It was one of those mountain mysteries I was able to solve, uncovering the kernels of truth that were becoming harder and harder to find as the years went by.

The reason for discovering the origins of the three sites mentioned in the previous paragraphs was to see if the exercise would provide some clues as to the origins of the Indian Steps. The Showers brothers, like Mr. Fox and Mr. Wagner, managed to build their extensive stone constructs using nothing more than bare hands; an impressive feat by any measure; and so it is certainly possible that one man could have built the Steps that lie on

---

4. J. Ernest Wagner (born November 9, 1910), recorded November 3, 1988.

Tussey Mountain. Certainly, natives didn't build them for military purposes, but it might be proposed that they built them to get to a particularly important ceremonial spot.

There is a small pile of stones at the top of the steps, and perhaps this tiny cairn had religious significance to the Indians. However, it could have been laid up in recent times, and if the aborigines did build the steps for this purpose, their exact reasons for doing so have been lost in antiquity. Likewise, if the steps were built as part of the extensive iron industry that once flourished in this area, the reason they were built has been lost over time as well.

Although Huntingdon Furnace (built in 1796) and the Coleraine Forges (built in 1810) were located near here, there is no evidence to suggest that the Indian Steps were built to support these businesses in any way. On the other hand, Tom Thwaites, avid hiker and father of the mid-state trail system, postulates that the owner of the land next to the iron company's lands on Tussey Mountain may have built the steps as a boundary marker to protect his real estate. The iron companies may have had a valid reason to build them as well, perhaps motivated by the same circumstances that led to the construction of yet another set of mountain steps in nearby Huntingdon County—the so-called Thousand Steps of Jacks Mountain.

The origin of the Thousand Steps is not cloaked in mystery like that of the Indian Steps. That's because the Thousand Steps are relatively young, having been created within the last seventy years. Built by employees of the Harbison-Walker Refractories Company in 1936, the stairway was carved out of the mountainside as a walkway for company workers to reach ganister quarries on the mountaintop. The stairs extend almost a thousand feet above the tranquil waters of the Juniata River as they flow through the haunted glen below.

Those who hike the seven-tenths of a mile to the top of the steps will find their efforts rewarded by commanding views of that wild glen, known to this day as Jacks Narrows in remembrance of Indian trader Jack Armstrong who was murdered here in 1744 (see the story entitled "Jacks Narrows" in the author's second volume in this series). Also, in the distance can be seen the small village of Mapleton, where many employees of the

Harbison-Walker Company once lived—the same workers who carved the steps out of the mountainside.

Employees of nearby iron companies could have built the Indian Steps on Tussey Mountain, just as Harbison-Walker employees built the Thousand Steps. Of course, it could also be suggested that the Indian Steps, and the stone cairn at their head, were the work of the same people that created the mysterious cairn-wall sites all over the east coast, including the one on Nittany Mountain called the Old Improvement or Council Rocks. However, none of the cairn-wall sites have stone steps leading up to the formations, which leaves us with a two-fold mystery in the case of the Tussey Mountain Steps. Like the cairn-wall sites, we don't know why the Indian Steps may have been built. We also don't know who may have built the Steps, whereas with the cairn-wall sites there is some historical basis suggesting the builders' identities.

Perhaps the Indian Steps are a unique example of a cairn-wall site, in that no others found to date have the added touch of stone steps leading up to the top. On the other hand, if the builders took the time and effort to build steps, it would seem as though there should be some rather impressive cairns and walls at the head of the stairs. You'd expect at least to find something beyond just a single small pile of stones. The more probable explanation for the small stone pile is that it was probably placed there by modern-day hikers as a trail marker.

So the steps themselves, perhaps, were the work of either iron company employees or of one man—the landowner there who felt he needed a clear demarcation line between his lands and that of the iron company which owned the adjoining property. However, there are those who would still like to believe that tribesmen built them, arguing that maybe the steps led up to a ceremonial spot so sacred that outsiders were never told about its significance.

Perhaps the Indians kept the secrets of this place so well that we shall never know for sure who built the steps. Was it a single individual, Native Americans, or ancient explorers who may have built equally impressive sites over the east coast? There are no clues to provide us a satisfying answer to the puzzle, but those who wish to delve further into the mysteries of this place can do what natives themselves might have once done—stand at the top of the Indian Steps and listen to the *Dah-gwa-nonh-en-yend*, or their Spirit of the Wind.

We would, of course, hear the wind if we stood at the top of the steps, but we would not expect to hear any answers as to who built them. On the other hand, there is peace and solitude to be found on the mountain, and also some magnificent views of the Bald Eagles and Alleghenies in the distance—enough vistas, in fact, to make the trek up to the Indian Steps a worthwhile endeavor, even though the origin of the steps themselves will probably always remain shrouded in the mists of the mountains.

NOTE: See the chapter titled "Stairways to the Stars" in the author's Sunbury-Press-published Pennsylvania Mountains Landmarks Volume I for more details about the Indian Steps, and a solution as to who built them after all.

NOTE 2: I was led to the Indian burial ground in Georges Valley, Centre County, while collecting legends and folktales in the area. Shortly thereafter, inspired by a hike up to the spot, I penned the following lines:

In the cool and shaded wildwood,
By a rushing stream
Lies a hidden resting place,
Where ghosts of Indians dream
Many wild things gather here,
A haven of slumber and repose
And this is the way it has remained,
For as long as anyone knows
But when winter's cold winds come,
And the ground freezes hard as stone
All creatures seem to shun this place,
Leaving it silent, and alone
Then in the springtime the peepers sing,
During the golden hour
And after sunset the night winds blow,

And stir this lonely bower
Some say that in Indian summer,
On nights when a red moon comes
You can hear a plaintive Indian song,
And the sound of distant drums
In autumn's cool crisp breath,
Under skies of deep blue haze
Leaves of yellow, brown, orange, and red,
Cloak the land in Indian maize
White smoke rises from a stone fireplace
Of the weathered log cabin nearby
While restless oaks and hemlocks,
Seem to moan and sigh
Across from the pleasant brown cabin,
In the shadows of old Egg Hill
There once was an Indian village,
But now it's invisible and still
It is the inhabitants of this village
That lie in the forgotten forest beds
And the only thing they've left behind
Are their legends, and black flint arrowheads.

NOTE 3: The author is also indebted to the following individuals for information used in this chapter:

Showers Steps: George Shollenberger (born 1933), Berks County, phone conversation May 1, 2001.

Georges Valley Indian sites: Wilber Confer (born 1905), recorded May 27, 1988. Clarence Lindthurst (born 1907), recorded December 17, 1986.

CHAPTER 2

GENERAL REYNOLDS'
SWEETHEART

O f all mankind's emotions, love is the most two-faced. On the one
hand it can produce boundless joy when it brings two people
together, but on the other hand it can lead to deep sorrow and great sac-
rifices when it is thwarted. It's not surprising, then, that stories and songs
about love and love affairs are often sad ones. The theme is, in fact, a universal one, extending back to the dawn of storytelling itself, and numerous
examples of the genre could be noted here. However, a song once popular in the Pennsylvania Dutch regions in the decades preceding the Civil
War probably conveys the poignancy of it all as well as any other ode or
lay. Composed in Germany in 1814, *In einem kiehlen Grunde* (In Yonder
Lovely Valley) tells the story of a lost love who will never return:

> In yonder lovely valley
> The wild mill-waters roar.
> My love, who dwelt there, vanished,
> I'll see her never more
> I'll see her never more
>
> She gave me a faithful promise,
> Gave me a gold ring, too;
> But soon her vow was broken;
> Then broke my ring in two.

I fain would be a minstrel
And wander far away;
And wander far away;
And sing in town and hamlet
My brokenhearted lay.

Were I a knight, I'd hasten
To join the bloody fight;
And by the campfire couching,
Seek rest in gloomy night.

That clatt'ring mill wheel's echoes
Strike woe into my breast;
I wish that I were dying,
Then all would be at rest.[1]

Loss of a true love for any reason is a hard pill to swallow, but it's probably hardest when that loved one is killed in battle. Many sweethearts have been lost over the centuries due to humankind's penchant for settling its differences by waging war, and yet the human race seems powerless to change its belligerent ways. If the atrocities of any single war could have helped to change those ways, it perhaps should have been the American Civil War. So many young men's lives were snuffed out in that conflict and so many terrible battles were fought that it would be almost impossible to find a skirmish where a faithful young lady did not receive news that she would never see her soldier boy again.

Such disappointments were apparently a common enough occurrence during the Civil War that Currier and Ives, the famous lithographers of that period, produced a lithograph that the bereaved could purchase to preserve the memory of their loved one. Entitled "The Soldier's Grave," the lithograph depicts a grieving young woman kneeling beside her beloved's tombstone, upon which could be lettered the name of the soldier, his regiment, and the place and date of his death. The author has one such lithograph in his possession, commemorating the death of Simon M. Stover, of A Company, 148th Pennsylvania Volunteers, who "Died at camp

---

1. George Korson, *Pennsylvania Songs and Legends*, 119-120.

Catherine Mary Hewitt. Major John Fulton Reynolds' "Dear Kate" and beloved sweetheart.

Major General John Fulton Reynolds. Highest ranking Union officer killed at the Battle of Gettysburg.

near Falmouth, Virginia on the 9th day of April, 1863." Then below the hand-lettered epitaph are these words:

A BRAVE AND GALLANT SOLDIER AND A TRUE PATRIOT
His toils are past, his work is done;
And he is fully blest:
He fought the fight, the victory won,
And enters into rest.

Certainly, one of the battles of the great American conflict that prompted Currier and Ives to publish their popular lithograph was the decisive struggle that occurred during the month of July 1863, at the Adams County town of Gettysburg. In terms of number of casualties, the battle of Gettysburg ranks among the highest of any battle of the entire Civil War, and it also holds the dubious distinction of claiming the life of one of the Union army's highest-ranking officers.

History relates how, on the first engagement of the first day's battle at Gettysburg, Major General John Fulton Reynolds was killed by a

Confederate sharpshooter's bullet. Reynolds, a native son of Lancaster, Pennsylvania, thus holds the dubious honor of being the highest-ranking Union officer killed during the three days' battle.

Given the outdated tactics used during the Civil War and the absence of rapid communications between commanders, it's a wonder that more officers were not killed at Gettysburg. General Reynolds, like his fellow generals, was often forced to make battlefield decisions without any knowledge of enemy strengths, or even where all the opposing forces were positioned. This sense of confusion in the middle of a pitched battle was often one of the prevailing emotions with which both Union and Confederate commanders had to deal, and the outcome of these Civil War struggles often hinged on quick decisions made on the basis of instinct rather than facts. Gettysburg was no different.

General Robert E. Lee had been concerned for some time about food and supplies for his troops, and he knew that one way to get those commodities was to make a bold invasion of northern territory. Lee also felt that any Confederate victory there might lead to an acceleration of the peace movements that seemed to be gaining momentum north of the Mason-Dixon Line. Moreover, England and France both might grant recognition to the Confederacy as a separate country if the south could achieve a big win on northern soil. With these goals in mind Lee decided to invade Pennsylvania, his main objective being the state capital at Harrisburg.

Lee's troop movements were eventually noticed by northern observers, and as the month of June 1863 ended, wave after wave of soldiers in the butternut or gray uniforms of the Confederacy and the blue of the Union were drawing toward one another in a blind rendezvous with death. It's said that Confederate General A. P. Hill had heard that a little Pennsylvania town called Gettysburg had a nice supply of shoes; and, since many of his men had none at all, Hill decided, on the morning of June 30, to send his corps after the badly-needed footwear (an apocryphal account that probably is more fancy than fact—historians say that, in fact, the armies blundered into one another, much to the consternation of the generals).

Two brigades of John Buford's Union cavalry had just ridden into Gettysburg. They were not here by accident. Buford was sent to the little country town by the newly appointed commander of the Army of the

Potomac, General George G. Meade. Meade was cautiously feeling his way around southern Pennsylvania, knowing that Lee was somewhere in the vicinity; and early on the morning of the thirtieth, several of Buford's advance troops spotted a line of dust on the Chambersburg Pike.

It didn't take Buford's men long to see that these were not Union brigades. Ragged and sunburned, many wearing mismatching uniforms and barefooted, the soldiers marching along the pike could, despite the dust, be readily identified as Confederates, and were in fact the men of Pettigrew's brigade, A. P. Hill's Corps. Buford's men opened fire, and, after a slight skirmish, Pettigrew's men were driven back, their muzzle-loaders no match for the breech-loading carbines used by the Union troops. However, the encounter gave Buford a chance to send word to Meade that there was probably going to be more trouble at Gettysburg the next day.

Neither Meade nor Lee wanted to get involved in a big battle at Gettysburg. Their troops were scattered, and neither side felt it was positioned well enough for a general engagement. But early on the morning of July 1, Buford's men saw another enemy column approaching. About three-quarters of a mile behind the column of advancing troops was a group of Confederate officers studying the situation. One Federal gunner spotted the officers and decided to take a shot. With the roar of his cannon, the battle of Gettysburg began.

Cannons started to roar to life on both sides, and the noise spurred Robert E. Lee forward to see what was happening. General John Reynolds' troops were just south of town, and they heard the thundering cannons too. Just then Buford's courier caught sight of Reynolds and gave him the fateful message, which caused the general to order his troops toward the sounds of battle. The Union forces arrived just in time. Buford's men were exhausted and were just about to be driven off Seminary Ridge by Harry Heth's division when Reynolds' troops counterattacked. Reynolds, realizing that the heights of Seminary Ridge was critical territory, sent a messenger to the rear, asking for reinforcements. His actions saved the day, but the gallant general could not save himself. A Rebel soldier saw the Yankee officer on horseback. Taking careful aim, the sharpshooter fired.

The Confederate onslaught proved too much for the Union troops, and they had to retreat southward through Gettysburg, finally digging in on Cemetery Ridge. Before the Federals retreated, however, they found their commander's body lying beside his horse. At first, they couldn't see what had killed him, but after lifting him up, Sergeant Charles W. Veil, Reynolds' orderly, noticed a hole at the back of the General's skull where a Minié ball, so named for the Frenchman who had invented it, had broken his neck when it hit the base of his brain. Called one of his "ablest officers" by General "Fighting Joe" Hooker, Reynolds' death was not only a great loss to the Union cause, but also was felt keenly by his troops, who had given him the nickname of "Old Common Sense."[2]

While inspecting his commander's body, Reynolds' aide, Major William Riddle, was struck by several oddities. Upon loosening the General's military blouse, Riddle noticed a silver chain around the dead officer's neck. Dangling from the chain was a medal from the Catholic Church, which struck the major as odd since the General was a Protestant. Also on the chain was a gold ring shaped like two clasped hands and engraved with the words "Dear Kate." However, most unusual was the fact that the General's West Point ring was missing from his finger.

The missing ring was something the soldiers could not explain. To a graduate of the Academy, the West Point ring is one of his most prized possessions. Those who wear class rings today don't know that the idea for them started at the military academy at West Point. A West Point class ring served as a seal of quality assurance to other officers on the battlefield, who knew when they saw it that the man wearing it was well-trained for his position. It was a piece of jewelry that was carefully guarded by those who were honored to wear it, and General Reynolds would not have been careless with his. Expecting to discover it among Reynolds' personal effects, Riddle and Veil were disappointed, finding instead several letters to the General from Torresdale, Pennsylvania (Torresdale Station is now part of Philadelphia). Written in a feminine hand, the letters were simply signed "Kate."

General Reynolds' body and personal effects were shipped to his sisters in Philadelphia, where the corpse would lie in state until July fourth.

---

2. Biographical information on General Reynolds: American Battlefield Trust, https://www.battlefields.org/learn/biographies/john-f-reynolds.

Biographical information on Mary Catherine Hewitt: Mary R. Maloney, "Mary Catherine Hewitt," *American Heritage*, December 1963.

On that sacred national holiday, the day commemorating the birth of this great nation, the general would be buried in his hometown of Lancaster. It was a hard blow to the General's sisters, Catherine and Eleanor, since they had been devoted to their brother. To lose him at age forty-two was almost more than they could bear, and they were glad to receive the personal effects his soldiers had brought them from the place where he had fallen. However, they were perplexed by the letters, and by the ring with its mysterious name.

To everyone who had known him, John Fulton Reynolds was a confirmed bachelor. His life, his love, and his lady had always been his military career, or at least that's the impression his lifestyle portrayed, and he had never mentioned anything to anyone about a special interest in any particular young woman. Yet here was evidence that he was deeply in love with someone named Kate, and so it was not a total surprise to the Reynolds sisters one day when a Miss Hewitt came calling and asked to view the general's body that was still lying in state in Catherine's house.

"Is it Kate?" inquired Eleanor Reynolds when she met the stranger at the door. After finding out that the pretty young woman was indeed the fallen officer's "Dear Kate," the tearful women spent hours together beside the General's body, getting to know one another and talking about the love affair that had up until then been a secret shared only by the soldier and his lady.

Today it's thought that Catherine Mary Hewitt met John Reynolds in California. Reynolds' army career included assignments to many different outposts in the nation, and it was when he was on one such assignment that he probably met the young lady from Oswego, New York, who had come west to serve as a governess for the C. R. Woodward family in San Francisco. It's not known when the romance between the two Easterners began, there on the west coast; but it had proceeded far enough by the time the Civil War was declared, that the two people had agreed to marry after the war and had even made plans for a European honeymoon. They also had a contingency plan in the event of a tragedy.

Catherine Hewitt returned to the east coast when John Reynolds was ordered back to serve in the war. He went off to do battle, after giving his West Point ring to his lady, but the young twenty-one-year-old governess

took an opposite path, entering a Catholic school in Torresdale and con-
verting to the Catholic faith. This was the plan that the two lovers had
discussed, agreeing that she would become a nun if he were to fall in battle.
Now that the worst had happened, Kate told the Reynolds sisters, this was
exactly the course she intended to follow. Deciding that she could not be
happy "in the world" without her beloved, Catherine Hewitt applied for
admission to a Catholic order. It was just eight days after John Reynolds
was buried.

The convent of the Sisters of Charity in Emmitsburg, Maryland, must
have seemed like the perfect place for the young newcomer. It was only
about ten miles from the exact spot where John Reynolds had fallen, and it
also had a direct connection to the man. It was probably that connection,
more than anything else, which caused Catherine to choose this order of
nuns over any others she might be considering at the time. If, on the other
hand, she didn't hear the story until after she had joined the Sisters of
Charity, then it must have been a pleasant surprise to her and a confirmation that she had made the right decision.

It seems that on the morning of July 1, 1863, the Union First Corps, led
by John Fulton Reynolds, had to march through Emmitsburg, Maryland,
on their way to their rescue of Buford's troops on Seminary Ridge. As fate
would have it, the marching men passed in front of St. Joseph's Academy.
This was to be the same school where Catherine Mary Hewitt would come
to study and to work with the order of nuns there known as the Sisters
of Charity. What greeted Reynolds and his men as they approached St.
Joseph's that July morning was a sight that none of them would ever forget.

"A long line of young girls led by several Sisters of Charity along the side
of the road fell upon their knees and with upturned faces earnestly prayed
for the spiritual and physical safety of the men about to go into deadly battle," recalled one account. It was a "solemn and inspiring" moment visibly
affecting even the roughest soldiers, who, along with every other man in
the Corps, took off their caps and kept their heads bowed until the prayer
had ended. And every man thought the prayers, coming from those sisters
of God and from innocent children, would be answered. It lifted their spirits and left them with one of their "sweetest memories" of the entire war.[3]

---

3. Herbert L. Grimm and Paul L. Roy, *Human Interest Stories of the Three Days' Battle of Gettysburg*, 42.

The good deeds of the Sisters of Charity didn't stop with the prayers for General Reynolds and his troops. The last day's battle at Gettysburg, July third, was on a Friday, and that night a heavy rain began to fall. The downpour continued through Saturday, turning the country dirt roads into thick quagmires. Undaunted by the road conditions, twelve of the sisters left Emmitsburg on Sunday morning with the intention of feeding and nursing the wounded. Along the roadways and in the fields beside them the sisters saw dead and dying Confederates who were left behind by a Rebel army that was struggling to retreat through the mud. The sisters may have stopped to administer to the Confederates as best they could, but their destination was the Gettysburg battlefield, and by the time they arrived there the day was turning hot.

Nothing in their experience had prepared the tender sisters for the sights they were about to behold. Bloated and discolored corpses of both men and horses were strewn all over the battlefield, the burial squads having just begun their work that same morning. Wounded men lay amidst the spent remains of war: cannons, swords, muskets, and bodies stacked two and three high. Puddles from the rains of the previous days were dyed red with the blood of the dead and dying. Over the whole sickening scene, the stench of rotting corpses filled the air. The sight was a horrible one, but the sisters were to see even more terrible things as they began to administer to the wounded soldiers.

Many men had been maimed beyond belief. Sister Mary David never forgot one particular soldier who had both arms and both legs ripped off by an exploding shell. In 1863 Sister Mary was in her early twenties, but the sight of the armless and legless soldier remained vividly imprinted in her mind until her dying day. Even in her old age she would recount the scene with a tremor in her voice. Although she would have preferred to have forgotten the sight, she would say "I can see him now after all these years, only the head and trunk of a man as they brought him in and leaned him up against a corner."[4]

What the Sisters of Charity saw at Gettysburg were sights too gruesome to forget, but it was not just women that were affected by the scenes of carnage. General William Tecumseh Sherman, the conqueror of Atlanta and the leader of the famous march through Georgia in 1864, probably

---

4. Gregory A. Coco, *On the Bloodstained Field*, 34.

described war best in his address to the graduating class of Michigan Military Academy in 1879 where he stated,

> "I am tired and sick of war. Its glory is all moonshine. It is only those who have neither fired a shot nor heard the shrieks and groans of the wounded who cry aloud for blood, more vengeance, more desolation. War is hell."[5]

The hell of war was not something that was new to the battle at Gettysburg. Men had fought wars for centuries prior to the Civil War, and for that reason it's perhaps not surprising that the story of General John Reynolds and his dear Kate is not all that unique. There is, at least, one interesting parallel to the Reynolds story that dates back over a thousand years, to the days of early German history when Charlemagne ruled his Frankish empire, and his nephew, Roland, was engaged to the most beautiful maiden along the Rhine, Hildegund, daughter of the Lord of the *Drachenfels*, or Knight of the Dragon Rock.

As fate would have it, Roland was summoned by his uncle to fight against the Moors before he could marry his beautiful Rhine maiden. According to the old Rhenish legend, Roland and his betrothed pledged to one another that they would either become husband and wife or they would renounce the world for as long as they lived. With this solemn vow in his heart, Roland went off to war. His deeds of valor were numerous, but during the battle of the Pyrenees he was so gravely wounded that reports of his death got back to his sweetheart. Crushed by the thoughts of the love that was lost to her forever, the faithful Rhine maiden joined a convent.

After a period of recuperation, Roland regained his health, and, with all the speed he could muster, returned to the Drachenfels to hold his love in his arms once more. However, much to his chagrin, he found out that she had been misinformed about his fate, and, true to their pact, had become a nun, joining a convent located on the nearby island of Nonnenwerth. It was more than Roland himself could bear, and he immediately renounced the world and built a hermitage overlooking the island where his love was forever isolated from him.

---

5. John Bartlett, *Familiar Quotations*, 613b.

Ruins of Drachenfels Castle on the "Dragon's Rock." View of the legendary castle as seen through Roland's Arch - along the Rhine, September, 1988. According to ancient Germanic legend, it was here at the Drachenfels or "Dragon's Rock" that Siegfried slew the dragon that made this place its home. According to the same tale, he then became invincible when he bathed in the dragon's blood. For decades a wine called Drachenblut (Dragon's Blood) has been produced by one of the many vineyards that can be found in this region. The author has one of the bottles in his personal collection.

Legend relates that he lived there for several years, and in all that time he only once saw the face of his loved one; the day when her fellow sisters brought her out of the cloister for burial. From that moment on the heart-broken prince lost all will to live, refusing all sources of nourishment until

Statue of Major General John Fulton Reynolds. Gettysburg National Military Park, Adams County. The horse's two raised feet indicate that the general was killed during the battle.

he passed away. It is said that when he died, he was gazing down upon the place which had claimed his bride, and which now held her lifeless body firmly in its grasp.[6]

Only a single arch of what is said to have been Roland's hermitage remains standing today. Clearly visible from the ruins of the Lord of the Drachenfels castle on the other side of the Rhine, the ivy-covered masonry is still referred to as *Roland's Bogen* (Roland's Arch) by the people of Germany who remember the old legend. Sitting three hundred and fifty feet above the river, it towers over the island of Nonnenwerth in the waters below. A convent was still thriving on the island at the start of the twentieth century, having escaped the ravages of Napoleon's army in the previous century when the French had maliciously eliminated other religious institutions along the river. It is said that Napoleon's wife, Josephine, interceded on the convent's behalf, thus saving it from destruction.

Perhaps Josephine knew the romantic legend connected with the convent at Nonnenwerth, and maybe it touched her so deeply that she

---

6. John L. Stoddard, *John L. Stoddard's Lectures, Volume VIII*, 94; Wolfgang Kootz, *Rhine Guide from Mainz to Cologne*, 92.

persuaded her husband to spare the place. Likewise, it is perhaps true that Catherine Mary Hewitt knew the legend of Roland and Nonnenwerth; and, like Napoleon's Josephine, was greatly inspired by it. It might be suggested, in fact, that the story may have been the basis for her decision to follow the same course as the Rhine maiden of the legend; that is, to enter a convent if her valiant soldier should die in battle. On the other hand, the similarities between the ancient legend of the Rhine and the story of John Reynolds' sweetheart may just indicate that in matters of war, love, and death, there are many parallels throughout history.

CHAPTER 3

CRY OF THE WOLF

"It is the most blood-curdling of all the noises of the night in the woods," claimed one early northwestern Pennsylvania settler when attempting to describe the dismal howl of a wolf. Even a small pack of half a dozen of the animals could, noted the same authority, "make the mountain seem alive for miles."[1] It was a sound not easily forgotten, and another early Pennsylvanian attempted to paint a word picture of the cry of a wolf pack in even more graphic language.

"I wish I could describe their howl," noted the Susquehanna County pioneer, struggling to find the words. "You would feel as though your hair stood straight on end when you heard it," he continued, eventually comparing the sound to that of a concerto of train whistles.

"Take a dozen railroad whistles, braid them together, and then let one strand after another drop off," said the man, recalling that the last strand of the music was the most terrifying of all. It was a chord "so frightfully piercing," remembered the old settler, "as to go through your very heart and soul."[2]

Another one of Northeastern Pennsylvania's earliest residents, also having heard the howls of a wolf pack in the wilds in the early 1800s, recalled that their chorus was accompanied by the "fine yelp" of the pack's pups. The combined "roar" eventually reached a level, the old man would later recall, "that seemed to shake the earth like thunder."[3]

---

1. William J. McKnight, *Pioneer Outline History of Northwestern Pennsylvania*, 119-120.
2. Emily C. Blackman, *History of Susquehanna County, Pennsylvania*, 281.
3. Ibid., 402.

"Bark cabin along west branch of Pine Creek above Corbett, Pa." Black Forest lumber scene – taken about 1898. (Photo courtesy of the Pennsylvania Historical Commission Public Relations Office, photo file RG-6, Dept. of Forest and Waters Pennsylvania State Archives #200.)

According to those same sources, not only were wolves unpleasant to hear, but they also were not the prettiest animals to see either.

"Coarse, gray-haired, ugly looking things," was the way one man would describe them seventy years after he had first encountered them in the Pennsylvania wilderness during the early 1800's.[4]

It was neither a sight nor sound that people wanted to experience in those days, when packs of wolves had their run of the mountains. During and prior to the last half of the 1800s, packs of wolves roamed freely over much of the state, decimating farmers' flocks of sheep and even being so bold as to attack belated travelers in the forest. During the last half of the nineteenth century and even into the first years of the twentieth, sightings of individual wolves were not uncommon in the less-settled parts of the state. But despite their prevalence and their audacity, the mighty packs that once roamed Pennsylvania's forests at will were gradually decimated by the state's settlers, who gave no quarter to the wolfish clan, until only a few lone survivors were left.

The decline of the wolf in Pennsylvania was a rapid one, due to the determined efforts of early mountaineers to rid the woods of the animal by poisoning and shooting it, and, according to some sources, due

---

4. Ibid., 281.

to widespread hydrophobia contracted from settlers' dogs. Whatever the causes, wolves were among the first of the state's original fauna to become extinct, disappearing from the mountains faster than even the mountain lion, and maybe that is why the cry of a lone wolf seemed both so sad and yet so menacing to those who heard it.

On nights when the melancholy light of a full moon penetrated even the darkest forest glens, the sound of a lone wolf's howl must have seemed more woeful than during any other night of the year. It was perhaps on such nights that the plaintive cry reminded people of a dirge, a mourning song sung in remembrance of the way things were before colonists had come, and, at the same time, a cry of defiance directed against those who were driving the wolf away from its native habitat. In any case, it was a sound that was long remembered, even decades after the animals were gone. The same, however, cannot be said for the stories about early settlers' thrilling encounters with wolves.

Unlike stories of encounters with mountain lions, which I could easily collect just thirty years ago, I found the tales of wolf encounters much more difficult to come by. The reason for this scarcity, I felt, was because wolves had been exterminated from the state much earlier than mountain lions, and so those who remembered the thrilling tales of Pennsylvania's wolf days had passed on before I could collect their stories. Nonetheless, I was able to find some episodes that I felt were worth recording, and they do seem to preserve a picture of just how trying life could be when settlers and wolves coexisted in the forests of Penn's Woods.

Several of these old-time wolf encounters have been recorded in the first four volumes of this series, and of all the tales I've collected I count them among my favorites. One of the reasons I suspect that is so, is because of the impressions they seem to evoke. In hearing the tales, or reading them again, I'm always reminded of the sweet fresh smell of the forest, the peaceful solitude of sun-dappled woods, the gentle whispers of playful mountain breezes, and the awe-inspiring views that are the reward of those who hike to one of Pennsylvania's lofty mountaintops.

These same stories, on the other hand, are also a reminder that the Pennsylvania mountains are much more interesting places because of the people who tamed them in the first place. To me the old wolf tales, more than any of the other types of folktales and legends, seem to bring us closer to those people and their colorful times.

If someone from that era of Pennsylvania history could be interviewed today, they would no doubt refer to that period as the good old days, but if pressed for details they would also recall that life in the mountains in those decades was not for the faint-hearted. Backbreaking work was required just to survive in the backwoods, but attacks on a farmer's livestock by mountain lions and wolves made survival even more difficult. Somewhat more worrisome was the ever-present possibility of an attack by those same predators on humans, and so backwoodsmen had to be ever vigilant, not only for the sake of their animals, but also for their own safety.

It must have seemed to those first settlers that they feared wolves more than wolves feared them. The nightly music of wolf packs often made the forest a forbidding place to be when the last rays of the sun disappeared behind distant hills. Even when inside their comfortable cabins, settlers would sometimes feel intimidated by the chilling chorus of a pack in full cry.

"The wolves would come near our cabin and make the night hideous with howling," was the recollection of one Susquehanna County pioneer whose father, in 1800, built one of the first cabins in the wilderness that was located near the present town of Dundaff ,and due west of a little local stream known in those days as Tinker Brook.[5]

Thirty years earlier the first settlers in Indiana County would also be serenaded nightly by wolf packs, since in those days, this part of the state was a favorite haunt of the animals. Not used to humans, and so still unafraid of them, wolves then could be unbelievably bold, as James Kelly found out one night shortly after he and Fergus Moorhead had finished building their first cabins.

The two men, who were among the earliest settlers near where the town of Indiana now stands, thought they could sleep comfortably inside their rough dwellings, safe from the elements and protected from the packs of wolves whose cries seemed to come from all sides as night fell. It turned out that the wolves, or at least one wolf, had other ideas.

One morning Mr. Moorhead decided to visit his neighbor's homestead, and when he got there, he noticed tufts of hair and drops of blood on the

---

5. Emily C. Blackman, *History of Susquehanna County, Pennsylvania*, 387.

The Decker Homestead. The log cabin home of John Decker that still stands today. It was in the field next to this cabin that Mr. Decker shot what some believe was the last native bull elk killed in Pennsylvania. He must have been serenaded nightly by the packs of wolves that made the Seven Mountains their home at that time.

ground at one side of the cabin. Not finding his friend about, Moorhead believed he had been killed by wolves and began searching for the body. Much to his surprise he found the missing Kelly nearby, sitting at a small mountain spring and washing the blood from his hair. Kelly, it turned out, had been attacked, but by a single wolf instead of an entire pack.

That previous night he had fallen asleep inside the relative safety of his cabin; but, Kelly explained, he was too close to a crack between the logs of one wall. Sometime during the night, a lone wolf had crept up to the cabin and saw the head of the sleeping settler just inside the opening between the logs. The gap was just large enough that the wolf could get its head through and seize Kelly by his head, and it managed to do so two or three times before awakening the unfortunate sleeper. Although his head was sore for some time, Kelly at least was still alive, and when telling others about this episode he always attributed his deliverance to the fact that the gap in the cabin wall was too small to allow the wolf to slip through it entirely.[6]

---

6. Sherman Day, *Historical Collections of the State of Pennsylvania*, 376.

Settlers in Miles Township of Centre County had similar experiences; and Anna Mary Geis, who was just two years old when her father Jacob brought his family from the Tulpehocken country of Berks County to Penn's Valley in 1798, remembered to her dying day how the wolves would howl around the very doors of their small dwelling, and how the animals' eyes "gleamed through the cracks of the cabin."[7]

In 1799 the area along Wyalusing Creek in Rush Township of Susquehanna County was full of wolves as well. This fact is perhaps suggested by the name of Wolf Creek, a little stream that flows through here and into Wyalusing Creek in neighboring Bradford County. Whether Wolf Creek was named from the prevalence of wolves here or not, stories handed down by the earliest settlers confirm that the animals, at that early time, could indeed be found here in substantial numbers. Surprised at their boldness, settler William Lathrop had to pile up wood in his doorway, which "had only a blanket for a door," in order to keep them out of his cabin at night.[8]

Several years later in Susquehanna County, Asahel Sweet's wife also had to find a way to keep the wolves out of her cabin. Captain Sweet sometimes left his wife and children alone for several days during the times when he was making sugar at his sugar camp; and one night when he was away a pack of wolves paid a visit to his homestead. Attracted by the smell of a freshly butchered sheep that the Captain had brought inside that day, the wolves silently surrounded the cabin. Alerted by the sounds of the animals "tramping around" outside, Mrs. Sweet began to worry that they might become so bold as to jump on the cabin's low sloping roof and come in through a hole that had been cut for a chimney.

Determined to keep the animals at bay, Mrs. Sweet kept a fire blazing under the hole, using handfuls of straw from the straw tick on her bed as fuel. Her defensive actions kept the wolves from jumping into the cabin through the hole in the roof, and at dawn she experienced "inexpressible relief" when she heard the animals disappear back into the forest.[9]

Ten years later in the same county, wolves were still scaring people, but Jonas Fuller "turned the tables" on a lone wolf he met in the woods one day near Elk Lake. Whether it was the thickness of the undergrowth or because both the millwright and the wolf had other things on their minds, neither

7. John Blair Linn, *History of Centre and Clinton Counties*, 363.
8. Emily C. Blackman, *History of Susquehanna County, Pennsylvania*, 216.
9. Ibid., 190.

saw the other until they were several feet
apart. Without hesitation, Fuller raised his
arms and yelled loudly at the animal that
blocked his path. Many years later, when he
was "up in his eighties," the old pioneer still
enjoyed telling the story of how his actions
that day scared the wolf that he had almost
stepped on. The ferocious looking beast was
frightened so badly, Fuller would relate,
that it just "turned and ran away."[10]

South of Susquehanna County, in
Luzerne County, about 1845, the wolves
weren't quite so easily frightened. Here,
in the Tomhicken Valley between Cataw-
issa and Hazelton, wolves not only preyed
upon farmers' livestock, but also frequently
attacked people as well. It was not a place
that a lone traveler would want to be at
night, but sometimes that happened, when
someone unfamiliar with the area got lost.

*He heard the wolves howl in old
Decker Valley. John Decker, born
1831, was the first permanent
settler in this remote mountain
glen and the valley was named
after him. (Photo courtesy of Mr.
and Mrs. Paul Wilson.)*

Dr. Thomas Thornton was fond of relating the story of how his father,
who was also a doctor, passed through this desolate region on his way to see
a patient one day and, confused by the dense undergrowth and rolling terrain, became disoriented. As the last rays of sunlight disappeared in the sky,
Dr. Thornton heard a pack of wolves nearby; and when the black curtain of
night finally covered the valley, he could see the eyes of the wolves glowing
in the dark as they approached him. Taking a bottle of ammonia out of his
medical bag, the quick-thinking doctor saturated one of his leggings with it
and used it to strike out at the wolves whenever they got too close. Repelled
by the strong fumes, the wolves were kept at bay, and the doctor used the
same defense against them the second night he had to spend in the valley
before finding his way out the next day.[11]

When no effective means of defense was at hand, people beset by
wolves had to find a place of refuge if they were to survive, even if it was

10. Ibid., 365.
11. Samuel N. Rhoads, *Mammals of Pennsylvania and New Jersey,* 151.

just the nearest tree. However, according to one tale that once circulated in the Seven Mountains country of Centre and Mifflin Counties, even a tall tree was not always a secure place when the wolves wanted someone badly enough.

"My mom told me this story, and she said her mom told it to her,"[12] recalled the ancient highlander. Born in the Zerby Gap in 1885, Clayton Auman could, in 1981 at the age of ninety-six, still recall the tales he had heard from those he called the "old people." The homestead where he was born still stands today in the little gap formed by First and Big Poe Mountains, and the old lumberman would have lived there until the day he died, except for a fall he had taken when he was there alone at the age of eighty-two. It was at that time that his relatives decided he had better leave his mountain home and come to live with them in the little town of Farmers Mills.

The old man had never heard or seen wolves himself when he was growing up in this isolated section of the mountains, but he still remembered the tale his mother told of one man who decided one day to "have some fun."[13]

She had heard the story when she was young, and so as the years went by, she recalled less and less about when the episode occurred, where it occurred, and the man's name that had the frightening experience. There was no doubt in her mind that the event took place "somewhere in the Seven Mountains," and that's entirely possible, since this was an area which remained almost entirely inaccessible up until roads were cut through these wooded ridges as part of the Civilian Conservation Corps programs of the 1930s. Since it was so wild and isolated, the Seven Mountains area was one of the last strongholds of the wolf in Pennsylvania.

Despite the difficulty of getting in and out of remote areas like this in the early times, there were still many people who preferred to be isolated from their fellow man so they could just enjoy the solitude of their remote mountain homesteads and the simple pleasures of life. No doubt the hero of the tale related by Mr. Auman's mother was one such person, and the kind of individual who in those days might have been described as an "antic sort of chap."

---

12. Arden M. Blunt, editor, *Gregg Township, Two Hundred Years Remembered*, 78.
13. Ibid.

Home of the old wolf hunter. Solomon Lingle's homestead and a view of the Zerby Gap, near the village of Greenbriar, Penn Township, Centre County. The road past the cabin leads south over Big Poe Mountain and into the wilds of Poe Valley. This area was once the home of many wolf packs, one of which surrounded Mr. Lingle early one morning in the 1850s.

Why the man thought it would be fun to excite and tempt a pack of wolves using himself as the bait was never fully understood; but he decided one day to apply a coating of animal grease to his shoe soles and then walk over a path he knew the wolves often used in their nightly excursions. Spotting a big, unusually tall tree beside the wolf path, the daredevil walked back and forth across the path at this point so as to leave a heavy scent. Satisfied that he had left a trail that would lead the wolves right to him, he then stepped behind the tree and awaited developments.

As night came on, wolves began howling in the valley below. The trickster standing behind the tree knew it was the cry of a pack preparing to go on a hunt, and soon he could hear them coming up the mountain. The wolves had picked up the scent of the animal grease on the man's shoes, just as he had hoped, and they now were on the old wolf path, a forest byway that probably had been used for countless decades by the ancestors of this same pack.

Solomon Lingles homestead at the Zerby Gap. A closer view of the old log cabin homestead, which is now hidden by modern-day aluminum siding. See the chapter titled "Wolf Days in Centre County" in the author's Pennsylvania Fireside Tales Volume III *for a thrilling story of Solomon Lingle's wolf encounter at this place.*

The cry of an approaching wolf pack could raise the hair on the back of anyone's neck, and if a harvest moon was in the sky, the kind typical of early fall when the moon is full and a gossamer veil of mist covers its face, the moonlight falling on the path would have been enough for the man to see the pack as it came into the clearing that surrounded the tree. It would have been enough illumination, in fact, that the sharp-eyed wolves would have seen the man, one of those beings they hated the most because they were their only predators, standing by the tall forest sentinel.

Deciding that it was no longer advisable to stay on the ground, the anxious watcher climbed into the safety of the highest limbs above. It was a prudent decision because the wolves soon emerged from the woods, running at breakneck speed but stopping when they came to the tree with its hidden observer.

Usually pausing at this point when he was telling the tale, Mr. Auman, realizing that the rest of the story would be hard for anyone to believe, would usually inform his listeners that "This is no story, this is the truth!" After providing that seal of authenticity, he would continue.

"Well, the wolves commenced to dig, and it was a big tree," claimed the old man, repeating the tale that, according to his mother, was based on a real incident. "They kept on digging at that tree until the roots tore off and the tree fell! It fell on another tree, and it was that straight that the wolves couldn't get up. They couldn't dig it out, but they didn't leave either. That man was up in that tree all that night! The next day his two dogs came looking for him, and they got rid of the wolves, and he could get down."[14]

Although Mr. Auman's tale sounds like one of the tall varieties, there are parts of his story that could certainly be true. Miss Blackman, in her interesting *History of Susquehanna County*, mentions several incidents in that region where the earliest pioneers were treed by wolves. In all these cases the people, including one woman, had to spend a night alone in a dark forest, either because they lost their way or were returning from a long trip and were unable to reach home before nightfall. Dismayed by the howling of wolf packs around them, the frightened travelers climbed trees as places of refuge, usually spending the entire night there.[15]

Similarly, in her fascinating accounts about the pioneer towns of Potter County, Mrs. Edythe Hancock recalls the fortitude of Mrs. Francis French of Oleona, who in 1843, was respected as "one of the hardiest of pioneer women." It was a title bestowed upon her because "she hunted, fished and trapped by her husband's side and sometimes even worked on log drives."

14. Ibid.
15. Emily C. Blackman, *History of Susquehanna County, Pennsylvania*, 435, 484.

However, the episode that probably cemented her reputation was the time when "she was in the woods alone with her gun and was treed by a pack of wolves." The hardy woman kept her head, firing "five times before her husband came to the rescue."[16]

These narrow escapes would have been terrifying and unforgettable experiences for even the boldest mountaineer. In the words of one man whose uncle was once treed all night with wolves howling at him from the ground below, it was a "greeting such as he never forgot while he lived."[17]

Philip Tome, the pioneer hunter of Pennsylvania's Black Forest country in Potter, Tioga, Lycoming, and Clinton Counties, had a similar harrowing experience one night while camping in a shanty along Big Pine Creek during one of his elk hunts. Describing it as "the most dismal night I ever experienced," he recalled how "wolves flocked around me in droves, and their unearthly howling, mingled with the dismal screeching of the owls overhead made a concert of sounds that banished sleep from my eyes the greater part of the night."

Alarmed by the danger, Tome "sat in my shanty, with my gun in one hand, a tomahawk in the other, and a knife by my side. When the wolves became too uproarious, I would send the dog out to drive them away, and if they drove him in, I would fire among them. At length toward morning, I fell asleep from sheer exhaustion, and slept until daylight, when I arose, ate my breakfast, and started again on the elk-track."[18]

Nighttime was the time when the wolves were boldest, but when the first hints of dawn appeared in the sky they became, in the words of one old pioneer, "cowardly villains," and would run back to their dens as though they were frightened by the revealing rays of daylight.[19] The fact that the wolves did have this timorous side to their otherwise fearless nature saved more than one person who spent a night in a tree wondering how they were ever going to escape the frightful animals howling up at them. There were others, however, that appear to have found unique ways to keep the wolves at bay even during the darkest nights.

---

16. Edythe Hancock, "Pioneer Towns in Potter County," *Historical Sketches of Potter County*, 211.
17. Emily C. Blackman, *History of Susquehanna County, Pennsylvania*, 195.
18. Philip Tome, *Pioneer Life; or, Thirty Years a Hunter*, 115.
19. Blackman, Ibid., 195.

In the account noted in a previous paragraph, Jonas Fuller claimed to have scared away a wolf just by shouting at it. It was a technique that was apparently an effective one, even for a woman. At least that's what Mrs. David Haney claimed, whenever she would tell of several encounters she had with wolves shortly after she and her husband settled in what is now Brady Township of Clearfield County in 1821. Remembered as a "courageous woman," Mrs. Haney would often recall the time when she also came face-to-face with a wolf late one afternoon when she was carrying one of her sister's children.

Instead of turning and running from the menace that was blocking the trail ahead of her and baring its teeth, Mrs. Haney stood her ground and "scolded him with energy to go home." It was apparently more than the wolf could bear, and the feisty lady was relieved when she saw it turn tail and "scamper off" into the dark and forbidding woods.[20]

It was a technique that the pioneer woman must have known would work, because once before she had used it, one night when her husband was away. During their first summer in the wilderness, Mr. Haney had been unable to finish their cabin. It had four sides and was under roof, but in the front, there was an opening where a door would eventually be put into place. Until they could close it off properly, the Haneys had hung a coverlet over the opening to serve as a temporary door.

On this particular night the wolves decided to attack the Haneys' cattle, and when she heard them Mrs. Haney threw open the front door and "resolutely scolded" the nocturnal marauders. Much to her satisfaction, and perhaps surprise as well, Mrs. Haney watched the cowardly pack turn tail and leave. Some nights later, after David Haney had returned, the wolves decided to come again, but this time the bold pioneer took his gun and went out into the dim moonlight. Taking careful aim he fired at the beasts. The shot scared them away, but he didn't know he had hit one until later, when he found its body in the woods nearby.[21]

Examples of two more alarming incidents just like this can be found in the story entitled "Wolf days in Centre County," in Volume III of this series. In that chapter is an account of a man being surrounded by a pack of

20. Lewis Cass Aldrich, *History of Clearfield County, Pennsylvania*, 460.
21. Ibid.

wolves in a remote mountain pass early one morning. Having no means of defending himself other than using a scythe he was carrying, the resourceful mountaineer managed to scare his attackers away by banging a sharpening stone against the blade of the scythe. Loud noises unfamiliar to the wolves were usually enough to scare even the boldest pack away, and this method of frightening them was apparently used quite often, with some surprising variations.

The story of at least one such episode was often repeated during the 1930s when a group of regulars would come to loaf at Andrew Rishel's store, a small country market that stood along the base of Tussey Mountain near the village of Tusseyville in Centre County. Rishel's establishment was the unofficial social club for many of the men who lived in the area; and regardless of the weather, Jess Taylor, Eddie Fryer, Sam Horner, Ed Zerby, and others could often be found here.

After making themselves as comfortable as they could on the old gray bench by the window, or on seats in other parts of the store, the men would talk of the things old-timers still talk about today when they come to drink coffee and loaf at little country stores that can still be found in small Pennsylvania mountain towns. Farming, hunting, fishing, politics, and family ties were no doubt favorite topics, but inevitably someone would have a yarn to spin, and it would remind someone else of another, and so the conversation would continue until it was time to go home.

In winter the men probably edged closer to the coal-fired stove that heated the store, but the cold temperatures never seemed to hinder the conversation as the best storytellers would entertain the others with accounts of ghosts, witches, hunting episodes and similar tales from the nearby mountains, including the one Datz Miller would tell about an unusual pile of stones over in his neck of the woods.

Datz lived in the nearby village of Colyer, which was located in that section of the mountains that locals still refer to today as the Loop. One of the stories that was once widely circulated in that area was the tale about the pile of rocks over in the Bear Meadows that didn't like it when anyone tried to take one of its stones. Whenever anyone tried, so went the tale, they could hear a noise like chains rattling coming from inside the rock pile. Although it sounded like just another tall tale, there were many who believed it, just like they believed Ed Zerby's tale about the pack of wolves that would follow him when he was helping to lumber off the nearby mountain.

Born in 1890, Zerby worked at a lumber camp over in Treaster Kettle, below Thickhead Mountain, in the first decade of the 1900s. Accommodations were not luxurious in any lumber camp, with hastily constructed bark shanties often serving as temporary homes away from home, and so most of the woods hicks looked forward to weekends when they could return to their families and sleep in more comfortable surroundings. Zerby was no different, working the entire week in the woods and then walking down off the mountain to the Zerby homestead that still stands today near the large sinkhole known as Tussey Sink. Thoughts of seeing his family again no doubt made his weekly walk something to look forward to, at least until a pack of wolves made the journey something to be feared.

According to the old lumberman, the wolves, which had to be one of the last, if not the last, packs in the area, became aware of his regular trips through the woods; and as time went on they became bolder, following him at closer distances each time. At first the lonely hiker didn't know what course of action to take, but one day when he was carrying a length of small chain, "the kind you might tie a dog with," he let it drag behind him when the wolves made their usual approach. Much to his surprise, the sound of the chain dragging through dead leaves lying on the forest floor was enough to keep his followers at bay. After that he carried the chain with him when he walked down off the mountain on weekends, and when the pack of wolves started to follow him, he let it drag behind him. It always had the same effect on them, or so said the old lumberman when he would tell his story to his rapt audience in Rishel's store, since the wolves would never get any closer to him than the end of the chain.[22]

One man who heard Zerby tell his wolf tale at Rishel's, remembers that he "told it many times," and it was always the same. There are others who doubt the story is a true one, since packs of wolves were supposedly eliminated from this part of Pennsylvania by the late 1800s. Moreover, Zerby's son says his father never told him this story and thought he would have done so if it had been a true one.[23] On the other hand, one old lumberman

---

22. Paul Rishel (born 1932), interviewed by phone July 31, 2000 and April 16, 2001.
23. Paul Zerby (born March 20, 1919), recorded August 6, 2000.

A lone wolf howling at the moon. A scene that was once quite common in our Pennsylvania mountains but which may be returning in more remote sections of our vast Pennsylvania forestland today. Solitary travelers hiking through a dark woods did not welcome this sound in the olden time, especially when dark clouds scudded across the face of a pale yellow moon and the night wind rustled dried leaves in the treetops. (Source: Postcard purchased from Zazzle.)

I talked to in my earlier collecting days claimed that "timber wolves" could still be found in this section as late as 1900.[24]

Wolves undoubtedly called this area home in the 1800s, but whether they were still here in Ed Zerby's day is debatable. Perhaps Zerby had heard this story about someone else dragging a chain to scare wolves away at an earlier time somewhere in the Seven Mountains, and maybe he just told the tale as though it happened to him so it would be more entertaining. Whatever the case, it would seem that at least the part about the chain could be based on fact.

Sometime in the earliest years of the nineteenth century, near present day Clarks Green in Lackawanna County, a pack of wolves made their home in Leggetts Gap, where Bald Mountain meets Bell Mountain and

24. Jared B. Ripka (born 1885), interviewed August 27, 1971 and February 2, 1974.

Leggetts Creek cuts between the two ridges. At that time there was a corn mill in nearby Slocum Hollow, and settlers living in the vicinity often carried sacks of shelled corn through Leggetts Gap on their way to get it ground into cornmeal at the mill. Oftentimes the wolves made any such trips harrowing affairs, because they would follow and sometimes attack anyone who trespassed into their territory.

Ebenezer Leach frequently walked through the Gap, going to and coming from the mill in Slocum Hollow, and he always carried a large cudgel which he would use to beat off the wolves that growled at him from all sides and sometimes tried to bite him. Although the clubs he used were often "bitten and broken," they were an effective means of defense, until someone told Leach that wolves "were afraid of the sound of iron." It was at that point that the brave mountaineer got himself a sawmill saw from a lumbering operation in the valley below.

In order to be able to drag the saw with one hand, Leach found a strong willow branch and tied it around one handle of the long blade. The flexible willow bough proved to be an ideal rope, and it allowed Leach to pull the saw along behind him as he traveled through the Gap. The noise the blade made as it clanged and clattered over stones and roots was enough to scare away the wolves. Their fear was so great, he would later recall, that his passage through the gap was now easier. He was never attacked by the pack as long as he was dragging the saw behind him, and the only other noise he could hear besides the saw was the "indignant" growling of the wolves as they watched him pass by.[25]

NOTE 1: There were apparently some wolves who seemed to have no fear of any man, or at least this seems to have been the case with a lone wolf which was one of the last of its kind killed in the Black Forest of Tioga County in the last decades of the nineteenth century. Its story appeared in the December 23, 1880, edition of the Wellsboro Agitator:

Two men were chopping wood in the woods near Westfield last Tuesday when they were surprised and very much frightened to see a large gray wolf coming towards them, looking gaunt and hungry, his white teeth glistening "in the bright light." They armed themselves with clubs, and

25. H. Hollister, *History of the Lackawanna Valley*, 277.

dispatched the animal after a most desperate struggle, and now Mr. Frank Eberle wants pay for his bulldog, which he recognized in the body of the wolf. [Presumably the payment Mr. Eberle had in mind was the bounty for the wolf, which was still being paid for wolf hides in Tioga County up to 1896.[26] JRF]

NOTE 2: In the genealogical records of Forest County there is an interesting and unusual account of how another man, whose last name was Smith, escaped a pack of wolves by skating faster than they could run. Although Smith's first name has not survived, the incident was recalled in some detail by early settler Daniel Harrington who settled in the Tionesta area in 1828. His recollection includes a first-hand narrative by the man who narrowly missed being ravaged by a howling pack of hungry wolves.

Harrington begins by recalling that, around 1820, two hunters had encamped near the spot which would later become the town of Newtown Mills, located in present-day Kingsley Township near where Rock Run flows into Tionesta Creek. The two adventurers had not only come to hunt but also to determine whether there was a sufficient quantity of pine timber to make it worth their while to invest in timbering operations, and whether the streams would be large enough to float the timber to market.

The only settler in the area at that time was Ebenezer Kingsley, and the two men set up camp near Kingsley's shanty along Tionesta Creek. It was here, one bright moonlit winter night, that the man named Smith decided to indulge in his favorite form of exercise. A recent cold snap had frozen the waters of the creek to a depth of three or four inches, and the surface was smooth and solid. The young man of twenty-three years had brought his ice skates along with him, and, after putting them on and satisfying himself that they were on nice and tight, took a few turns in front of their camp to be sure they were securely fastened before starting out for a run of a few miles up the creek.

He told his story to Mr. Harrington, who later recorded it for posterity, telling it in the words of the young man as closely as he could remember them, as follows: "I had gone perhaps two miles up the large stream. The night was almost as light as day and very calm. I could hear the echo of the ring of my steel skates on the shore as I passed swiftly along. Coming

---

26. Samuel N. Rhoads, *Mammals of Pennsylvania and New Jersey*, 154.

to the mouth of a smaller stream on my right, I concluded to explore it a short distance. It was very crooked. In going up it some three quarters of a mile, I think, I must have traveled fully two miles. Its average width was about sixty feet.

"Both banks of the stream were heavily timbered, principally with hemlock, and the branches interlocked forming a complete canopy over my head, making it quite dark in comparison with the broad creek I had just left. How long I might have enjoyed the delight of the exercise and the beautiful scenery of this little stream I cannot tell.

"Then I was unpleasantly interrupted by a strange sound which I supposed at first was the hooting of an owl. As I listened the conclusion came to me that the noises came from wolves and boded me no good. Keeping my presence of mind, I started on the back track for the mouth of the creek. I had not gone far before I heard the howls unpleasantly near. In my race for safety, I had to follow the course or the windings of the stream, while my pursuers traveled not more than half the distance that I was forced to get over. It was a race on my part for life, and for supper on the part of the wolves. To make a meal for a gang of those savage animals is not a pleasant prospect.

"At about forty yards from the mouth of the little creek they tried to head me off from the big stream. The bank was quite a bluff, and I could see them on shore ready to spring upon me as I passed. I bent my head and brought every nerve in play in the effort to pass this point of danger. As I passed under full headway they jumped at me, but miscalculating my speed they struck the ice quite a distance behind.

"I glided out onto the broad Tionesta, and felt relieved, but the race was not over. They followed me on down the stream. I was perfectly at home on skates, but all my fleetness and skill were necessary to enable me to escape their fangs. When they came so near that I could hear their pattering on the ice I would wheel to the right or left and gain upon them, for they could not turn as short as I could but were compelled to keep on for several rods before they could change their course.

"By this maneuver of frequent tacking, I kept out of their reach until our camp was in sight. We had two dogs chained up in the shanty, and when they began to bark and raise an uproar, the wolves turned back, and I was safe. How long the race lasted I do not know. It seemed an age but was probably not more than an hour—perhaps not so long as that. Had one of my skates got loose or had I tripped on a stick, this story would have never been told by me!"

According to Harrington, it would seem to him that from Smith's description of the little stream and its zigzag course near its mouth, he undoubtedly went up Salmon creek, which empties into the Tionesta fourteen miles from its mouth and two miles above Newtown. Today the area where this episode occurred is called Kingsley Township in honor of Ebenezer Kinsley, its first settler, and it's located in the Allegheny National Forest. This same history of Forest County also adds some further confirmation as to the truth of Smith's story by noting that "At the mouth of Big Coon creek, six miles above Tionesta, was a great crossing for deer and bears. The wolves used to run deer in on the ice and kill them, so that the traveler could often see carcasses on the ice."[27]

27. J. H. Beers and Company, *History of the Counties of McKean, Elk, and Forest, Pennsylvania*, 828-858.

CHAPTER 4

THE BEWITCHED BUTTER
CHURN

"Cherries, that used to be our snack on Sundays," recalled the lady, describing her life in the mountains during the first decades of the twentieth century. Born in 1905, the white-haired storyteller was now eighty-three, but her memory of the old days was unimpaired, and she held a group of us spellbound as she told us of her life while growing up in a little-visited valley located near the Seven Mountains country of Centre County.

"We didn't have candy, not like the kids do today, but we'd make homemade ice cream sometimes," she informed us, then described just how they made this delicious treat. "As soon as we'd get a snow, why then we'd take cups and put sugar in and either cocoa or vanilla and milk. Then we'd take spoons and go out and get some clean snow and mix it up 'til it got thick."[1]

She went on to tell us more fascinating episodes from a time that preceded the current year by eight decades, but her account of how she and her siblings made small servings of homemade ice cream by mixing milk with flavorings and snow was one of the most pleasant memories we took away with us when we left her that day. It was a reminiscence we would think of again the following month when we heard another narrative about the difficulties someone else had when attempting to make homemade ice cream with a hand-cranked freezer in the 1930s.

1. Gladys Brown (born December 15, 1905), recorded April 23, 1988.

"Anybody ever tell you about Sammy Lingle?" queried the son of the lady who had told us about how she had learned to make homemade ice cream using freshly fallen snow. We had to affirm that we had never heard of the gentleman he mentioned, and with that the retired farmer, who had begun farming in 1948, told us about an episode that occurred around 1936 in the Loop area near the small village of Tusseyville, Centre County.

"Old Sammy was up at John Bubb's place one night, and they were making ice cream with a hand freezer," explained the life-long resident of the same valley where his mother was born. "They turned and they turned, and they turned, and they turned, and he said it wouldn't get hard. Then here come old Sammy.

"He said, 'Uh huh, you're making ice cream without me?'

"John's dad, his name was John too, said, 'It won't get hard!'

"Sammy said, 'I'll fix that', and he took the lid off and took a butcher knife, went down in the ice cream, mixed and stirred around, and talked, you know, said some things. What he said, John don't remember, but then he put the lid on 'er."

"John said in no time they had ice cream. He said that son of a gun could do more than make ice cream!"[2]

John Bubb's comment that Sammy Lingle "could do more than make ice cream" was a variant of a veiled expression (the most common form was "could do more than eat bread") used in those days, and in previous decades, to indicate that someone was either a hex (a bad witch who was always tormenting people or animals by casting spells that made them sick or prevented them from accomplishing something) or a *braucher* (a good witch who could counteract the spells of a hex.) In this case the Bubbs believed that a hex's spell was what prevented their milk from turning to ice cream and that Sammy Lingle was a braucher whose mysterious actions and words had successfully counteracted that spell. It was no doubt a belief that had come down from previous generations who once held the deep-seated notion that a hex would often bewitch their wooden butter churns so that the cream inside would not turn into butter, no matter how long or how hard they churned.

The account of one such episode was once a popular tale in Georges Valley, Centre County. Thirty years ago, the little valley formed by First

---

2. Harry Brown Jr. (born 1926), recorded May 5, 1988.

*An old-time wooden churn. Used in the days before
electricity came to mountain homesteads, these manually
powered wooden devices were used to churn cream into
rich butter.*

Mountain and Egg Hill in the foothills of the Seven Mountains was a place
where you could still hear many accounts of brauchers and witchcraft,
and it was here I collected my first folktales, including the story of the
"bewitched butter churn."

No doubt the story of the bewitched churn was once a favorite folktale
that was repeated and embellished whenever people talked of such things
in the nearby towns of Potters Mills and Spring Mills. It was an anecdote
that was always guaranteed to spellbind a listener, and probably was once
a juicy piece of gossip that adults carefully whispered to one another if

children were present. Evidence of its popularity is the fact that, sixty years after it occurred, I could still talk to people who remembered the story and who had personally known the parties involved.

There was, in fact, one person still living who had seen the mysterious profile formed by droplets of cream that had splashed out of the

Aunt Susie Crater's hexed butter churn. And the sheet of paper covered with odd designs and symbols that Aunt Susie had drawn upon it and then placed beneath the churn to counteract a hex that a local witch had put upon the churn to keep Aunt Susie's cream from turning to butter—my staged representation of what it must have looked like.

churn and onto the brown piece of paper underneath. But it was in an old antique shop in Georges Valley, Centre County, one dark and dreary day that I first heard the tale from another man who liked to tell the stories of a bygone era.

Early one rainy morning in late August 1971, I was driving along the Upper Georges Valley Road when I noticed a sign for Zettle's Antiques at the entrance to a gravel lane that descended to a farm nestled, and almost hidden, amidst rolling hills in the valley below. I had been to the shop before, and now decided that this might be as good a place as any to start collecting the kinds of tales I was looking for. I turned on to the road and soon came to a large red barn with a low wooden shed next to it. Above the door in the front of the weather-beaten building was an aging sign with the word Antiques painted on it, so I got out of the car and went inside.

As I entered the shop I was greeted in a friendly manner by Lester Zettle, owner of the shop and long-time antique dealer. We chatted for a while, and I finally explained to him the reason for my visit and the type of stories I wanted to hear. Without hesitation he told me to "wait once," and with that he went to the back of his shop. Soon he reappeared holding a yellowed piece of lined tablet paper with some words penciled on it, which he invited me to read as he handed it to me. As I began to inspect the faded inscription I was immediately puzzled by the meaning of the sentences, which read as follows:

> Trotterhead, I forbid thee my house and premises. I forbid
> thee my horse and cow stable. I forbid thee my bedstead,
> that thou mayest not breathe on me; breathe into some other
> house until thou hast ascended every hill, until thou hast
> counted every fence post, and until thou hast crossed every
> water and thus dear day may come again into my house, in
> the name of God the Father, the Son, and the Holy Ghost.
> Amen.

"Years ago, I used to find quite a few of these papers when I was invited into different homes in this area to appraise or buy antiques," explained the valley native. "They were called witch papers," he noted, "and they were placed over the front doors of houses or behind the horseshoes they used to nail above barn doors for good luck. People thought these things would protect their families and livestock from a witch's spell," he continued, with a far-away look in his eyes that revealed his fondness for the past.

It seemed that this reminiscence was the catalyst the antique dealer needed to recall some of the witch tales he had heard throughout his years of buying and selling the relics of previous decades. As he began to entertain us with some of the stories, we suddenly realized, as we listened to him, that our surroundings couldn't be more appropriate for hearing someone relate tales of witches and *hexerei*.

The light rain that had been falling all morning was still coming down from the lead-colored overcast sky; and glancing out the back windows of the dimly lit shop, I could see plumes of heavy white mist rising off the Seven Mountains to the south. Here and there the bare branches of dead or dying trees could be seen clawing their way out of the mist, and the raucous cries of crows could be heard in the fields nearby.

Inside the shop, an ancient grandfather clock with a moving moon-faced dial ticked away contentedly in one corner of the room. Antiques of all kinds hung on the walls or sat on the shelves around us, including old farm tools, ornate kerosene lanterns and valuable stoneware crocks with rare blue designs decorating their sides. Together they formed all the accoutrements that should be present when tales of the long ago are being told, and they seemed to make the antique dealer's stories even more enjoyable than if they had been told in more modern surroundings.

Perhaps it was the loud cawing of the crows outside that prompted the antique dealer to choose as his first story an old witch episode that he recalled from many years ago. He began by describing how a room in an old farmhouse in the valley supposedly once filled with crows when a local lad perused a passage from a large tome of black magic lying on a table in the same room. The boy's father heard the commotion, so went the tale, and running into the room he commanded his son to "read it backwards, read it backwards," whereupon the boy recited in reverse the passage he had just read. It was the correct counterspell to cast, at least according to the old story, for it caused all the crows to immediately fly back out the open window that they had used as an entryway.

The antique dealer's tale had whetted my appetite for hearing more of the same kinds of anecdotes before I went back out into the rain, and my interest must have been obvious to the old storyteller. Convinced he had an avid listener, he went right into his next account. Even more intriguing than the first, it was the tale of a woman who could not churn her cream into butter until she resorted to supernatural means.

The setting for the events recalled by the folktale is in a valley which, up until the last forty years, was still largely unsettled. Even just fifty years ago, John Decker, the valley's first settler and the man for whom it's named, would have found the place almost unchanged from the time he built his log cabin here shortly after the Civil War. It was in a field in back of this cabin, according to local legends, where Decker shot the last native elk in the state.

Years after the old settler's death, the area remained a good hunting ground, and eventually a group of nimrods turned the old place into a hunting lodge after they bought it from John Decker's heirs. Now falling into a state of disrepair, the weather-beaten Decker homestead stands as a reminder of those earlier days when people's lives were simpler, their pleasures few, and stories like that of the bewitched butter churn were accepted as fact by those who heard them.

Back in those days people had strong opinions about who the local hexes were and the diabolical mischief they could cause. In the mountain homesteads in and around Decker Valley, for example, it was once widely believed that Carolyn Confer was one such person, and it was also generally accepted that it was she who bewitched Susan Crater's butter churn one day.

Aunt Susie Crater had never had a problem churning her cream into butter before, but on this afternoon "it wouldn't make." The experienced housewife was perplexed, as were all the other women who were there helping or visiting on this day. The ladies must have discussed the situation, and how to remedy it, and no doubt some of their recommendations were tried; but, if so, none resulted in the cream turning to butter. It was at that point that Aunt Susie announced that she would "fix it," whereupon she went inside and came back out with a plain piece of brown paper. As she placed it under the churn some of those standing closest noticed that the paper had sentences written on it, words which appeared to be a counterspell.

The preparations were not yet complete, at least according to some versions of the tale, because the determined woman next asked the others to get "buggy lines" (the leather straps used as the reins and harness when horses were hitched to horse drawn carriages) and to place them in a circle around her. The onlookers did as requested, bringing the leather lines from the barn nearby and carefully placing them around the old lady who was standing by the bewitched churn. Once the circle had been formed to her satisfaction, Aunt Susie solemnly announced to the others, "Now I'll get butter!" and commenced churning again.

There are those who say the cream turned to butter almost immediately, while others say Aunt Susie waited until midnight to start churning again, and then when the cream was turning to butter it "rumbled like thunder." But all accounts do agree that while "Suse" was churning, some drippings from the churn fell onto the paper below. Eighty years later Roy Zettle, brother of the Georges Valley antique dealer, still remembered what he saw when he took a closer look at the congealed drops of cream.

"I saw the picture under the churn," recalled Mr. Zettle. Born in 1896, the old man had many interesting tales to share, but this one seemed to be one of his favorites. "Now whether it was just imaginary or not, I don't know, but it looked like an old woman bent over like this," he explained as he hunched over to illustrate what he had seen. "That's an old witch story," proclaimed the witness to the strange event.

When pressed for further details, the friendly storyteller had to admit that the picture was not distinct enough to be a likeness of someone he or anyone else could recognize. The only reason people thought that the image was of Carolyn Confer, he confessed, was because that was "just who Susan Crater told us it was!"[3]

The old fellow's confession seemed to indicate that putting a "spin" on an event was not a technique invented by today's shrewd politicians to make people interpret things in a way that's favorable to the statesman's image or hidden agenda. Instead, it would seem that the old-time brauchers and hexes were not above using the same technique to impress others. Rather than discourage any further dialogue by pointing out this fact, I let

---

3. Details provided by the following individuals: Charles Braucht, recorded November 17, 2001; Jared B. Ripka (born 1885), interviewed August 27, 1971 and February 2, 1974; Roy Zettle (born 1896), recorded June 23, 1990; Randall Steiger (born 1904), recorded June 4, 1982 and May 4, 1988; and Lester Zettle (born 1914), interviewed August 27, 1971.

the entertaining octogenarian continue, but he had nothing further to say about the bewitched butter churn. However, his antique dealer brother had told us there was a sequel to the old narrative and had related it to us that day we first heard the story in his antique shop.

It seems that shortly after Aunt Susie had cast her counterspell and proclaimed that Carolyn Confer was the hex that had bewitched her butter churn, the accused came calling. The visit was not entirely unexpected, at least for Aunt Susie and others who believed in the powers of witchcraft.

In those times when the greatest power of witchcraft was the hold it had on people's minds, it was accepted as fact that if a braucher's counterspell was successful, then the hex whose spell had been nullified would suffer extreme pain, and her agony would continue unless she could borrow something from the person she had tried to torment. It was an ancient belief, and the basis for the last part of the bewitched butter churn story, which describes what happened when Carolyn Confer appeared on Aunt Susie's doorstep one day and asked if she could borrow some sugar, because she was baking pies and had run out. The conversation that followed was supposed to have gone like this:

"No, I don't have no sugar myself," replied Aunt Susie, whereupon her visitor tried to borrow some salt, professing to be out of that as well.

"My salts all too," replied Aunt Susie, knowing that Carolyn was trying to get loose from the counterspell that had been cast upon her.

What the rest of the conversation between the hex and the braucher was, is no longer remembered today, but it is recalled that Carolyn was able to outwit Aunt Susie by furtively picking something up as she left the premises. By doing so, she was released from Aunt Susie's counterspell, but perhaps she had learned her lesson. Aunt Susie apparently never had a problem churning butter afterwards, or at least there are no other valley folktales that say she did.[4]

Belief in spells and counterspells had ancient roots, and it was a notion brought to Pennsylvania in the 1730s by German immigrants from picturesque valleys along the Rhine River and from legend-laden glens of the Schwartzwald. It is not surprising, then, that tales of bewitched butter churns could once be found in any part of Pennsylvania where the Germans settled. The superstition was an oft-repeated part of the folk wisdom

---

4. Lester Zettle (born 1914), interviewed August 27, 1971.

of their culture, and the saying "If the butter won't come, the milk is bewitched; to drive out the witches, put red-hot iron into the churn," was not uncommon advice in Pennsylvania Dutch land.[5]

Dutchmen down in Fulton County had similar beliefs, which are preserved in an account of a woman there who would take the cream out of her bewitched churn and heat it on her wood stove until it came to a boil. Then, while crisscrossing sharp knives through the boiling cream she would order the hex or the hex's spell to "get out and stay out." By performing this ritual, she was convinced that she was not only driving the witch or witches away, but causing them harm as well, with the end result being that the witch could be seen the next day with scratches all over her face, caused by the sharp knives slicing through the boiling cream![6]

Further east, beyond the Blue Mountains, the same ideas once circulated among the Pennsylvania Dutch in Berks County. A popular notion there at one time was that a counterspell for cream that was not turning to butter was to pour the cream on a hot stove. Although the cream would be wasted, the action would, it was thought, discourage the old hex who had bewitched it not to try it again. This idea is preserved in one folktale from the area that relates that when one family tried this very thing "it became known the next day that an old woman had been badly burned by falling against her stove."[7]

Up in the coal country of Carbon County, the remedy was to pour some of the bewitched cream into a bag full of flour and then beat the bag with a heavy stick. Further south, in Lancaster County, some people felt that even if their churn was not bewitched, they could increase their yield just by putting a red rag into the churn. However, in this case there was a price to pay, and it was higher than most people would want to spend. This approach, it was thought, would make the devil appear with his book of souls, which he had tricked people into signing so they could prosper while in human form. Lucifer's price, it was said, was that any person who signed his book also forfeited their soul to the Black Prince.[8]

---

5. John T. Faris, *Old Trails and Roads in Penn's Land,* 71.

6. Edwin V. Mitchell, *It's an Old Pennsylvania Custom,* 179.

7. Thomas R. Brendle and William S. Troxell, "Pennsylvania German Folk Tales, Legends, Once-upon-a-Time Stories, Maxims, and Sayings," *Proceedings of the Pennsylvania German Society, Volume L.,* 106.

8. Dr. Alfred L. Shoemaker, "Folklore and Legends of Lancaster County," *Lancaster Intelligencer Journal,* November 11, 1948.

Statue of the Lorelei. Preserving the legend of the Lorelei, the water nymph of the Rhine, this monument sits on a small island in the Rhine River near the village of Oberwesel—taken by the author in 1988.

Belief in bewitched butter churns eventually faded away as the superstitions brought from the Old Country were replaced with modern methods and thoughts, but the process was a slow one. I was reminded of this fact on the same day that the antique dealer had informed me about how people once believed that witches could prevent their cream from turning to butter.

The antiquarian's wife had come into the shop shortly after I arrived, and she seemed to enjoy hearing the story of the invading crows as much as I did. As I was copying down the inscription that was penciled on the witch paper, she cautioned me in all seriousness to "read it backwards" if the copied passage I was taking with me caused my car to fill with crows. I assured her I would, but, of course, nothing like that happened. However, it never occurred to me to call her and let her know that, and I'm sure she went to her grave believing that it could have.

CHAPTER 5

TALES FROM ALONG
THE TRACKS

Sometimes late at night, when the night wind blows in from the north, my wife and I can hear the lonesome wail of a train whistle and the clickity-clack staccato of train car wheels as they pass over steel rails. The first time we heard the nocturnal sounds, we were at a loss to explain where they were coming from. They seemed to rise from the valley floor below us, even though there are no train tracks running through Halfmoon Valley, so the out-of-place noises left us momentarily perplexed. However, it didn't take us long to realize that the train we were hearing was rolling over the railroad tracks that pass through the valleys and towns beyond the Bald Eagle Mountains—the ridges that form the northern boundary of the little valley named after the half-moon carvings early settlers found on the trees here. The rugged mountainous terrain is formed in such a way that sometimes the winds carry the train sounds through gaps in the mountains and over to us. The pleasant echoes always seem to be those of a phantom train, and when I hear them, I'm often reminded of the tales that I've included in this chapter.

Remembered in Greek mythology as bird-like maidens who lived on an uncharted island in the Ionian Sea, the Sirens sang their hypnotic songs for the same reason a spider weaves its web. Unable to resist sailing toward the sound of the sweetest singing they had ever heard, mesmerized seafarers supposedly ignored, or did not see, the sharp rocks surrounding the island,

Along the tracks of the Bald Eagle Railroad. From an old postcard titled "Coming around the turn into Bellefonte, Pa.," scenes like this were once commonplace in the Pennsylvania mountains during the era of steam trains and steel rails, but now they are only faint memories.

and steered their vessels right into them. As their ships slowly sank into the ocean, the last thing the drowning sailors heard was the beautiful voices of the deceitful enchantresses that had called them to their deaths.

The Lorelei in German mythology was another such witch; a hex who was said to lure sailors to their deaths with her hypnotic songs. Long ago it was believed that this beautiful seductress made her home along the narrowest and deepest place in the Rhine River, between the towns of Kaub and St. Goarshausen. Here, sitting on a ledge of the large slate cliff that was the cause of so many shipwrecks, the Lorelei sang out her charming tunes, and it is here today that a statue of this beautiful assassin still works the same magic, causing tourists to stop and take its picture.

To some men, the shriek of a train engine's whistle is like a Siren's song, or the song of the Lorelei who haunts the cliffs of the Rhine. There's something about the lonesome wail that is alluring to those with wanderlust, inspiring them to venture forth and experience the freedom of riding the rails. It's almost as though the trains themselves are like the irresistible Sirens or Lorelei rather than the victims of these mythological creatures. At least there seem to be no tales of train wrecks attributed to a Siren's song or stories of train engineers being hypnotized by eerie music coming from supernatural beings that haunt the rock ledges along the tracks. On the other hand, there are accounts indicating that ghosts do haunt the rails, and that they sometimes are not always quiet or shy about revealing themselves.

One person who knew many such tales from along the tracks of what was once the Lewisburg, Centre, and Spruce Creek Railroad was Sam Ryder. The feisty World War I vet was employed by the railroad as a track-walker, and it was the only job anyone knew Sam ever had. He may have tried other jobs before landing this one, but the duties of a trackwalker seemed to blend best with his temperament. Sam was a loner, and he didn't mind the solitary nights he spent walking the five miles of steel rails that stretched from Coburn in Centre County to Poe Paddy, near the Centre and Mifflin County border, and back.

Maybe one reason for his seeming indifference to the rigors of his occupation was that whenever he walked the tracks Sam had to concentrate on his duties. His job was to inspect the tracks, especially those inside the tunnels, for debris or damage that might cause the train to wreck. He was also charged with removing any debris he found on the tracks. It took a special man to do the job; a man who didn't mind the loneliness, or who could ignore the weird sounds of the night that often came from the deep dark forest on both sides of the tracks. The nocturnal life of a trackwalker was certainly not for everyone.

Not everyone could motivate themselves to perform this same task every night of the year, regardless of weather conditions, and not everyone might be able to remain convinced that belief in the ghostly world was only held by those who had not advanced to more sophisticated ways of thinking. Perhaps it was the loneliness that caused Sam to be more attuned to the supernatural than most people, or maybe it was his innate super-stitious nature. On the other hand, the hardened veteran of what came to be known as the Great War, that great European conflict during the years 1914 to 1918, might have seen and heard things during his lonely nocturnal strolls that made him a believer after all.

Exposure to uncanny surroundings and bizarre noises on a nightly basis could tend to wear a person down; could influence the way they thought about the world around them and about the unseen world as well. And it cannot be denied that these influences would have been stronger on those foggy nights when thick white clouds of mist dancing in yellow beams of moonlight seemed to fill every ravine and every gap in the mountains through which the steam locomotives passed. On such nights it would have been particularly unsettling to see one of the trackside graves that sometimes could be found in unexpected places along the rails.

Such graves were not uncommon in Pennsylvania, many of them the final resting places of workers who were on the crews laying track, and who died from illness or injury on the job. Unmarked gravesites like this are said to be located beside the tracks of what was once the Pennsylvania Railroad's main line near the town of Frazer in Chester County. Interred in these forgotten resting-places along here are the remains of several railroad laborers who died of cholera about 1830.

Sam Ryder may have passed by similar interments as he walked along the tracks from Coburn to Poe Paddy in the wee small hours of the morning, but if he did, he never let it bother him. The old trackwalker kept to his task for many years, until one day he finally decided to retire and spend his time hunting and fishing—the two activities he enjoyed the most. On the other hand, perhaps what really prompted the faithful employee to step down was a realization that his days with the railroad were severely numbered anyway.[1]

More modern ways of doing things were continually being implemented by the railroad, and the trackwalkers were eventually replaced by section men, who inspected the tracks while riding on handcars—those small flat-bedded cars with a hand lever which the riders would pump up and down to propel the car along the tracks. While the new ways of doing things no doubt impressed many people, they did not have the same effect on the ghosts which haunted the tracks. New innovations created new specters, just like the one that could once be heard riding a phantom handcar on the Pennsylvania's tracks along Penn's Creek, between the country towns of Spring Mills and Coburn.

The tale of the phantom handcar was never widely disseminated outside the remote section where the story arose, but the source of the uncanny sounds seemed to like it that way. The noises only occur late at night or in the dark hours of early morning at one particular spot along the tracks, and

---

1. Mr. and Mrs. Jake Fryer, recorded September 13, 1997.

so they are only heard by those who have a good reason to be here at this lonely place during that time, like the anglers who counted this part of the creek as one of their favorite fishing holes.

Sometime in the early '60s, the two fishermen came here to fish for eel, and, as they had often done in the past, brought lanterns with them, intending to fish until midnight or even later. It turned out to be a foggy night, and as darkness fell, the light from the men's lanterns created a surreal yellow glow as it was dispersed in the evening mists. The eerie surroundings didn't deter the determined anglers, and they continued to fish, seemingly indifferent to or unconcerned about things of a supernatural nature. Suddenly, however, that attitude changed when one of the men heard what he thought was a train coming down the tracks that ran along the other side of the creek.

"I knew it wasn't the train, because the train wasn't runnin'," explained the fisherman, recalling that evening's events. "I set there, and I kept hearin' it; just like wheels clatterin'," he explained, "and then I looked over at him [his fishing buddy] and I said, 'What the devil is that?' He started laughin' and said, 'That's a handcar! Didn't you ever hear that before?' 'Hell,' I said, 'there's nothin' runnin' on that track,' but he said, 'I'm tellin' you that's a handcar, and it'll never get here!'

At that point the second angler demanded an explanation, and so there along the creek, while the flickering lantern lights cast strange and unsettling shadows on the opposite bank, where the trees swayed and whispered in the night wind, he heard the tale of the phantom handcar for the first time. But, before beginning the odd narrative, his companion dramatically pointed to a large pile of rocks on the other side of the quiet stream and asked a question.

"See that rock pile over there?' he queried, to which his curious listener replied that he did indeed see the large pile of stones. "Well, one time two fellas on a handcar got into a fight, and the one pushed the other off. He was killed when he landed on that stone pile over there," continued the first man, recalling the old story that he had heard years ago. "And now if you're up here on a certain night when it's foggy like," continued the storyteller, "sometimes you'll hear that thing comin', but it'll never get here!"

Still not convinced that his fellow angler was telling the truth, the intrigued listener suggested they stay there awhile so he could see if his midnight companion was just having some fun with him or not. The men stayed there until 1:30 in the morning, and the doubting Thomas finally had to admit that his friend's statement was a true one.

"It never got there!" he recalled, as though he was still hoping that someone might have a reasonable explanation for what he had heard that night. Still doubting his own senses, he obviously felt he needed to put some sort of closure on the event in his own mind, and also in ours. "A fella can hear some weird noises, I'll tell ya!" he concluded, stating the obvious. However, he knew as well as we did that this was really no explanation at all, and the strange occurrence left him perplexed to his dying day.[2]

Sam Ryder would have agreed with the angler's comment about weird noises. One of the trackwalker's favorite stories, and one which he often told, was the tale of the screaming tree. According to those who heard old Sam tell the tale, sometime in the late 1800s, shortly after the railroad tracks had been laid, a young couple moved into this remote area, building their homestead near the first railroad tunnel outside the small village of Coburn. The wife was pregnant, but for some reason the expectant parents decided to abort the birth. The procedure went as planned, and afterwards the couple hid the aborted fetus in a hollow tree which stood near the entrance to the long dark tunnel. However, the couple hadn't planned on the fact that the child's spirit would be a restless one. Ever since that time, claimed Sam, screams that sound like those of a young child can be heard coming from the hollow in the tree on the night that is the anniversary of the fetus's placement there.

Many people today, of course, doubt whether those screams could ever be heard at all, but if such noises once did break the silence of the forest along the tracks on that same night every year, it's questionable if they still do. Likewise, there are others who express the same reservations about the sounds of the phantom handcar. Basis for some of the skepticism is the fact that about thirty or forty years ago the steel rails along this section of the Pennsylvania Railroad were taken away, victims of the hard times that had fallen on the once powerful company, leaving only the wooden crossties. This, say the skeptics, was probably enough to lay any ghost whose spiritual essence was somehow tied to the rails, but there are others who disagree.

---

2. Ray Rowles (born 1933), recorded May 26, 1988.

Although the steel rails are no longer there, and the wooden crossties have slowly rotted away, the railroad bed on which they were placed is still evident. But with the passing of every year the forest is slowly reclaiming the ground, erasing even this reminder of the trains that once came this way. Still, at least one restless spirit seems not to have been affected by these changes, and perhaps other vapory essences that once haunted these same tracks weren't either.

In addition to the unquiet phantoms that may still haunt the same places that they have haunted for the last one hundred years along the now-missing tracks, there is another ghost that may still do so as well. This spirit is not a noisy one, preferring to remain silent as it carries a lighted lantern on its lonely nocturnal wanderings. But despite its silence, anyone who is unfortunate enough to encounter this "terror that comes in the night" is as badly shaken as those who are scared by the noisier revenants. After all, an encounter with this spirit would terrify someone as much as Washington Irving's fictional hero Ichabod Crane was frightened, when he met the headless horseman of Sleepy Hollow.

Like the tale of the phantom handcar, the story of the headless ghost of Sinking Creek is a well-kept secret. Only a few people remember it today, and the reason that it has not been forgotten entirely is because some of those who have seen the headless spook are still living and are willing to talk about what they saw. It's a narrative that could have been concocted by any good storyteller, and this was the way I would have regarded it myself, had I not been convinced otherwise by one person who encountered the horrifying specter near the spot along the tracks where it was decapitated when in human form.

Up until about twenty-five years ago encounters with the headless spook occurred on a regular basis. Since that time the restless spirit seems to have gone dormant, apparently content for a while to savor the last time it frightened someone. As far as is known, that occurred one dark night back in 1975. It was a night in early spring, at the start of fishing season, and two young fishermen had not had much luck. The fish did not seem to be biting that night, in that stretch of Penn's Creek that runs along the creek road between Spring Mills and Coburn; and soon both young fellows became bored and told the man they were with that they were going to follow the creek road into Spring Mills and then come back. It was only about a half-mile walk into town, and it would have been an uneventful stroll had the boys, once they got into Spring Mills, gone back the way they had come. However, the fifteen-year-olds decided to walk back on the railroad tracks that ran along the opposite side of the creek.

It was a moonless night, and the two adolescents could hardly see as they made their way along the tracks and the night continued to darken. Then, by the time they were halfway back, between Spring Mills and the old log cabin that still sits near where the road from Millheim crosses a bridge over the creek and continues its way into the wilds of Poe Valley, it was almost pitch black. It was at this bridge that the boys and Bob Meyer had agreed to meet, and although it was almost pitch black, the fellows were unconcerned, knowing that if they stayed on the tracks they would eventually come to the bridge. Then, in the woods beside them, they noticed what appeared to be a light from a lantern. At first the pallid glow piqued their curiosity, especially when they noticed that it seemed to be following along with them.

The mysterious light seemed out of place, but then one of the boys proposed that it was just Bob Meyer trying to scare them. His companion didn't agree, pointing out the fact that Meyer would have had to drive his truck up to Spring Mills and then walk rapidly back along the tracks until he had caught up with them. It was not likely that their heavy-set chaperon could have accomplished this feat, and besides, recalled one of the boys, "there was no lantern in the truck!"

At this point the young fishermen picked up their pace, but bolts of fear shot through the lads when they saw that the light was moving along with them at the same rate of speed. Confident that, as hardy fifteen-year-olds who could run like the wind, they would soon outdistance the eerie light if they began to sprint, the boys made a mad dash down the tracks, only to see the light keeping up. What was even more disconcerting was that the person, or whatever was carrying the lantern, never made a sound as it moved through the brush and trees beside the tracks. Then, as suddenly as it had appeared, the light was gone, just as though someone had blown it out.

Stopping to rest, and not knowing what to do next, the frightened teens both got out the hunting knives they were carrying and stood motionless, as though frozen to the tracks. Gasping for breath, the terrified adolescents carefully looked around to see if the light was still there. Calming himself down, one of the boys decided a more methodical search was in order. He first looked back down the tracks they had just passed over, and then he looked to his right, then to his left, and then in the direction they had been running. He could no longer see the mysterious light and was just about to breathe a sigh of relief, when he turned around to look back down the tracks one more time. There, about fifteen feet away, was the dark silhouette of what looked like a full-grown man. In the shadowy figure's hand was a lighted lantern, which the motionless apparition appeared to be holding up in front of itself to find its way along the tracks.

The spectral form seemed to be standing there looking at them, as though contemplating its next move, and the boys strained to get a better view of their pursuer. The faint glow of the lantern hardly penetrated the inky blackness of the night, but it was bright enough to illuminate the eerie figure that was holding the lamp; strong enough that the boys could see that the figure had no head! The sight froze the two young adventurers to the spot and momentarily left them speechless, but as their senses returned, they began to scream and holler at the menacing shape, hoping to scare it off.

The frightful cries and shrieks that penetrated the dense thickets of the adjacent woods, and which seemed to echo through the dark ravines of nearby Egg Hill, did not produce the effect the boys had hoped for. At that moment the ghostly shape began to move toward them, and, to their alarm, they could see that it didn't seem to be walking. They could see no movement of the being's vapory legs as it glided along like a cloud in the sky being driven by a gentle wind. Feelings of sheer terror prompted the swift-footed teens to turn and run once more. As they did so they both dropped their hunting knives on the railroad track.

Like frightened rabbits, the fleeing youths ran as if their very lives depended upon it, and as they fled, they glanced over their shoulders to see if they were outdistancing the horror that wanted to catch them. It was an even race for about twenty-five or thirty yards, and then when the boys looked back once more, the apparition was gone!

The ghost's disappearance wasn't enough incentive to slow the runners down. It wasn't until they saw Bob Meyer at the old bridge that they reduced their pace somewhat. When he saw the trembling boys who looked white as sheets, Meyer's first reaction was that they had been scared by something. When the panting youths excitedly told him that "some guy" had just chased them, he became concerned, asking the pale-faced teens if they had gotten a good look at their pursuer.

"Well, you're gonna think I'm crazy," declared the young man who had gotten back to the bridge first, "but the guy had the lantern up and he didn't have a head!"

"Bob, I didn't see no head," confirmed the second boy.

"We saw shoulders, but we couldn't see a head!"

"You know what? You probably ran into our ghost!" exclaimed the valley native, after pausing a moment to consider what he had just been told.

Both young men immediately wanted to know "what ghost?" and it was then they heard the story of the headless switchman who forever walks the tracks along Penn's Creek.[3]

Although the details are sketchy and the man's name is no longer known, all who remember his story agree that the switchman was decapitated near the spot where the two young men saw his restless spirit on that dark spring evening over twenty-five years ago. The accident occurred on a similar dark night, in a year that has also been forgotten, when the switchman was switching the tracks to route an oncoming train toward the mountains to the southeast.

The distant sound of the freight cars clicking over the rails may have alerted the switchman that the train was ahead of schedule, and perhaps that caused him to work faster and less carefully than he would have otherwise. In any case, in his rush to execute a "flying switch," he somehow got caught in the tracks. Then, to make matters worse, in his struggles to free himself he knocked over the small railroad lantern that had provided him with the light he needed when he was shifting tracks. As the light went out and rolled out of reach, the trapped switchman could only listen and then watch in horror as the oncoming express came into view.

There are those who say the spirit of the unfortunate switchman still haunts the tracks because he cannot rest until he finds his head. But if so, then he is not alone. Stories of headless spooks were once favorite railroad

---

3. Nedra Meyer, recorded June 6, 1999; David Prout (born 1960), recorded June 6, 1999.

yarns that were told about other places along the tracks of the Pennsylvania Railroad, one notable example being that of another switchman who was decapitated along the rails of the famous Horseshoe Curve at Kittanning Point above Altoona.

Moreover, accounts of headless ghosts are a favorite motif in the entire realm of folktales and legend; they have always been and probably will always be as popular as tales of phantom freight trains, ghostly carriages, and spectral ships. They either will be remembered as long as people enjoy hearing about them, or until the ghosts themselves find eternal peace.

NOTE: Apparently, the headless ghost of Penn's Creek is not content to rest upon its laurels any more after all. One summer night in 2001 it surfaced once again, surprising a late-night traveler who was hoping to see some deer that evening.

It was midnight, and the moon was full, when the young nighthawk left the bowling alley in Millheim and got into his truck to drive home. After reaching Spring Mills, he passed through the deathly quiet village and turned right onto the Sinking Creek Road to head towards Potters Mills. It was a sultry night in July, and the heat prompted him to roll down his windows; but he probably would have done so even if it hadn't been so hot. He liked to watch for deer when traveling along here after dark, and with the windows down he could listen for any of the nocturnal animals stirring around in the woods beside the road. This night, with his windows open, he reduced his speed so he would have a better chance of hearing any noises along the roadway. His patience was soon rewarded with the distinct sounds of rustling in the brush to the left, on the creek side of the road.

Listening carefully, he kept hearing the sounds, thinking the whole time that they were coming from deer in the brush beside the railroad tracks and in the bushes along the opposite side of the creek. Although he hoped to see some nice animals, something didn't seem quite right to the listener, and as a feeling of uneasiness began to rise up within him, he began to wonder why deer would be in the creek at that time of night. At about that same time he was nearing the old railroad bridge that crossed over the roadway several miles west of Spring Mills. When he looked across

The Headless Ghost of Sinking Creek. It was an apparition like this that two Boy Scouts say they encountered one dark night along the tracks of the former Lewisburg, Centre and Spruce Creek Railroad, later purchased by the Pennsylvania Railroad. The tracks are no longer there, but the railroad bed can still be discerned in places.

the creek there, he noticed what appeared to be the flickering light of a lantern back in the woods, and after passing under the bridge he noticed that the light was now in the woods on the right side of the road.

The illumination was now more distinct, and it was evident it wasn't coming from someone's flashlight. At that point the situation was so unnerving that the amazed observer began to wonder if the unnatural presence would try to jump onto the back of his pickup truck. Deciding it would be best not to hang around to find out, the truck driver increased his speed from thirty-five to fifty, only to see the light keeping right up with him. It was a harrowing confrontation for a while, but about a mile from the bridge the light disappeared just as quickly and mysteriously as it had first appeared. After he told me about this experience, I, in turn, told the man who had seen the eerie light about the legend of the decapitated switchman. He had not heard the tale before, and he was amazed when he realized that he was now one of a select group who had seen what some believe is the light from a lantern carried by the Headless Ghost of Penn's Creek.[4]

4. Tom Henry (born 1984), phone interview March 11, 2002.

CHAPTER 6

TOM COLEMAN'S REVENGE

Standing along a little-traveled byway in the picturesque Sinking Spring Valley of Blair County, just a short distance east of the site where the old fort known to history as Fort Roberdeau once stood, is a well-preserved stone building that was also used as a fort in an earlier day. The small village of Arch Spring has grown up around the sturdy fortress since that time, and the area is now included in the National Register of Historic Places, but the history of the Arch Spring fort itself has somehow been sadly neglected.

With its heavily barred windows and gun ports on two sides, the structure was undoubtedly designed to be used as a place of protection against Indian attacks. But, just like the swirling sparks in the smoke from an Indian campfire, memories of any such attacks have faded away, along with the older generations who might have remembered the stories of the place or any details about the people who were once associated with it. The old peoples' accounts, had anyone taken the time to record them, may have even prompted historians to treat the Arch Spring stronghold with more respect, thereby saving it from becoming just another forgotten part of Pennsylvania's storied past.

Many of the state's frontier forts have not withstood the test of time as well as the Arch Spring fort. Even the great Fort Roberdeau could not outlast the persistent forces of nature that eventually will always obliterate traces of structures that humans, for one reason or another, have decided not to maintain. But like the proverbial Phoenix, a new Fort Roberdeau has arisen from the ashes of the original.

In recent times interested citizens of the area have reconstructed a full-size replica of the old fortress, and a visit here, especially during those halcyon days of an Indian summer, affords a pleasant walk back into the past for those who like to experience a flavor of those times and their trials. Just several miles east, on the other hand, the Arch Spring fort stands almost forgotten, widespread knowledge of its existence languishing for almost a hundred years, because mention of it was never included on the pages of any histories of the area.

Even the five members of Governor Pattison's commission, appointed in 1893 by the state legislature to locate and document the sites of Pennsylvania's frontier forts, did not include the Arch Spring bastion in their final report. They may be excused for this oversight because it was decided at that time that only forts built prior to 1783 would be acknowledged as the true frontier forts of the state.

The 1783 cutoff date meant that the Arch Spring fortress, which was built by Jacob Isett in 1788 and is thereby most accurately referred to as Fort Isett, did not qualify as worthy of inclusion in Frontier Forts of Pennsylvania, the two-volume work that was the ultimate product of the 1893 commission.

Local historian J. Simpson Africa, author of the *History of Huntingdon and Blair Counties Pennsylvania*, published in 1883, even fails to mention Fort Isett in his extensive work, probably because the bastion was built seven years after the last documented Indian incursion into Blair County in June 1781, and so had little to offer in the way of thrilling tales of the Pennsylvania frontier. It is the details surrounding this last Blair County attack that led to another forgotten episode in the annals of Pennsylvania's Colonial period.

The murderous ambush of a party of rangers not far from the mouth of Sugar Run in June of 1781 resulted in the deaths of seventeen of the brave frontiersmen, who are now known to history as the Bedford Scouts. Details of the incident tend to be sketchy, and accounts differ, but most agree that this corps of frontiersmen were from what was then known as Fetter's Fort, a substantial stockade located near the present-day Blair County village of Eldorado.

Fifteen of the rangers were killed immediately in the ambush, and two others were captured and scalped. The fortunate survivors rapidly scattered

Remains of Fort Isett. Built for protection from Indian attacks in Sinking Spring Valley of Blair County. It was built seven years after the last documented Indian attacks, and so never had to withstand such warfare. It sill sits silently today near the small village of Arch Spring.

in different directions and would live to see another day, including hardened frontier-men Thomas and Michael Coleman, two brothers who already harbored an intense hatred of Indians because of an earlier ambush that claimed the life of a third Coleman brother.

The westward expansion of Pennsylvania's frontier during the time of its Indian wars was usually spearheaded by that fiercely independent people known as the Scotch-Irish. Appearing to be almost antisocial to less adventurous pioneers, a Scotch-Irishman did not like to settle too close to his neighbors. So well-known was this trait that a tenet of the times was that if a Scotch-Irishman could hear his neighbor's hounds he then knew it was time to move west to less-crowded conditions.[1] However, the Scotch-Irishman's aloofness arose from more practical reasons rather than

---

1. Mrs. Frances Thornton, "The Scotch-Irish, Pioneers of the Pioneers," *Centre County Heritage, Volume 4 – No. 1,* April 1968.

Distant overview of Fort Roberdeau. Built by early settlers to guard nearby lead mines, the original fortress no longer stands, but this remarkable replication gives visitors a sense of what it must have been like to live under conditions of siege warfare.

from antisocial ones, not the least of which was the desire to limit the competition for the wild game animals which served as a pioneer family's main source of meat. But it was this unrelenting western expansion that raised the wrath of the natives as well, for they still considered territory that had not been purchased by the provincial government to be their best hunting lands and a primary source of food.

The strategy of keeping a substantial buffer zone of dense wilderness between themselves and other settlers meant that the Scotch-Irish would move into Indian territory before the colonial government and the natives who laid claim to the same lands had reached an agreement allowing any encroachments. It was almost impossible for the colonial government to prevent such trespassing, and despite their best efforts, the most notable example being the burning of settlers' cabins in the Big Cove in May of 1750, the westward movement took on a momentum of its own.

Today the Fulton County town of Burnt Cabins sits close to the Fulton—Huntingdon County line several miles east of Fort Littleton and near

Main entrance into Fort Roberdeau. The main gate of the fortress with some of its interior structures beyond.

Side view of Fort Roberdeau. Showing its sturdy log posts used in its construction.

Little Aughwick Creek. The name Fort Littleton preserves the memory of the frontier fort that once stood on this spot, just as the name Burnt Cabins serves as a reminder of the fearless Scotch-Irish frontier families whose homes once stood here before being burnt to the ground by colonial authorities. Typical of their people, the Burnt Cabins families must be given credit for their bravery, but there were other borderers who were even better known for their seeming lack of fear when it came to pushing their way into hostile territory.

While many of the annals about the adventures of these bold frontiersmen had been long forgotten when histories of the state were being written in the late 1800s, there were others that were waiting to be told by members of the older generation who had heard their parents and grandparents speak of Pennsylvania's Indian wars. Unfortunately, many of these elderly folks never got a chance to pass on their recollections to those who were preserving a record of the state's past for future generations; but that did not stop the old storytellers from orally sharing the accounts with their children and grandchildren, who, in turn, shared them with theirs. In this way a small number of little-known episodes from the dark and bloody days of Pennsylvania's Indian wars did, like Fort Isett, weather the storms of time, even though historians had passed them by.

It was one of these almost-forgotten episodes that was passed on to me one day in the early 1970s when I was making my first efforts to preserve some of the state's folktales and legends. Although part of the story had been recorded in an early history of the Juniata Valley, the valley's oral history of that same episode included more details about the incident that caused Thomas and Michael Coleman, the two brothers mentioned at the start of this chapter, to become implacable foes of all Indians.

Notable among Pennsylvania's staunch Scotch-Irish pioneers and the other settlers who were in the forefront of the expansion into the wild and unsettled interior of the state were several sets of brothers whose reputations as Indian fighters seemed larger than life. Among this group of men, over in what is now Clinton and Lycoming Counties, were Samuel and James Brady and the Groves, Peter and Michael. On the Blair and Huntingdon County frontier the Beattys, Kriders, Ricketts, and Moores, family units consisting of seven brothers each, were also fearless foes of the Native American sons of the forest, and, in the words of an historian of the area, were considered "the most formidable force of active and daring frontier-men to be found between Standing Stone and the base of the mountain."[2]

At the same time that the Beattys, Kriders, Ricketts, and Moores were defending the frontier settlements of present-day Blair and Huntingdon Counties, the Coleman family, including brothers Michael and Thomas, was living on the cutting edge of that frontier, near where Spruce Creek drains into the Little Juniata River, present day Huntingdon County. In some ways the Colemans' Spruce Creek lifestyle would today be considered idyllic, but it was also a life strained by the fear of Indian attacks and clouded by sorrowful memories of a son who would never return.

There should have been a third Coleman brother living with the Colemans at their Spruce Creek homestead. His name has not come down to the present day, either through written or oral history, but the story of his murder by Indians one fine spring morning when the sap was just starting to run in the maple trees seems to have been one of those unforgettable events that left an indelible mark upon the annals of the West Branch and the Juniata.

Prior to moving into the Spruce Creek region, the Coleman family had lived somewhere to the east along the Susquehanna River's West Branch, and it was here that occurred the unfortunate episode that claimed the life of the third Coleman brother when he and his two brothers were busily employed in boiling maple sap into syrup one day in 1763. Shortly after lighting the fire under the large iron kettle containing the maple sap, one of the Coleman brothers discovered bear tracks in some soft ground nearby. Quickly it was decided that the two oldest brothers, Michael and Thomas, would take up the chase, while the youngest Coleman would stay behind to attend to the boiling cauldron.

The trackers followed the bear's trail for several hours but were never able to catch up with the wily creature. Frustrated and tired, the brothers agreed that it was time to return to their sugar camp. A brief account of what they found when they got there is recorded in Uriah Jones' remarkable

---

2. Uriah J. Jones, *History of the Early Settlement of the Juniata Valley*, 279.

annals of the Juniata Valley, but the oral history of the region once contained more specific details of the grisly event.

One day in May, in 1974, perhaps a day not unlike the one on which young Coleman was murdered, I was privileged to hear the oral history of that event, recalled to a group of fascinated listeners by a Juniata Valley centenarian who had grown up hearing the old folks of his younger days tell and retell tales of the region's border warfare. Among those tales was an account of the younger Coleman's murder, and another about how Thomas Coleman surprised a group of Indians himself one day.

The year 1763 ushered in the start of many gruesome scenes of burning cabins and scalped settlers in Pennsylvania's frontier regions. This last forceful attempt to dislodge colonists from Indian lands became known as Pontiac's War, named after the chief who was its organizer and leader. Although the uprising failed in the end, it was the cause of many deaths on the frontier, and it might have been some of Pontiac's warriors who caught the youngest Coleman brother alone by his maple syrup kettle. Although he no doubt put up a valiant struggle, the young frontiersman was no match for the determined band of strong warriors.

When the other two Colemans got back to their sugar camp they were greeted by a depressing and sickening sight. Sunk into one of the wooden props supporting the iron kettle was a tomahawk, red with the gore of its recent victim. Upon closer inspection the dazed woodsmen found the contents of the kettle still boiling, and included in those contents were the jellied remains of their brother. In a state of what must have been a mixture of rage and disbelief, the grieving brothers buried the remains as best as they could, broke up their camp, and returned home with the sad news. Shortly thereafter the Coleman family abandoned their West Branch homestead and moved to the Juniata Valley.

It was this incident that turned the two Colemans from frontiersmen who harbored a strong dislike of natives to confirmed Indian haters who vowed that they would seek revenge for their brother's gruesome death until their dying day. Folktales of the Juniata Valley indicate that at least Thomas Coleman did not break those vows, and one story in particular preserves a belief about how far he would sometimes go to slake his need for that revenge.

After telling us the story of the younger Coleman brother's murder during maple syrup season of 1763, the old gentleman who was entertaining us with many accounts of the long ago surprised us by relating a sequel to that dismal episode. It was a tale he had heard as a young man and one that had only been preserved by becoming part of the oral history of Blair County.

"One time Thomas Coleman was trailing some Indians through the mountains," began the wizened and white-haired storyteller. "He thought they were ahead of him, but he eventually realized that they had worked their way around behind him," he easily recalled, as though he had just heard the story yesterday.

"After backtracking a ways, he laid down beside the trail and covered himself with leaves. It was snowing pretty hard, and so he let the snow cover him up. Soon the Indians walked by in single file, and after they passed, he jumped up and shot at them and his musket ball passed through and killed several at one time. The others scattered and ran.

"Later he saw a fire on one side of the river. He knew the Indians were using it as a signal fire to guide them back to their camp. He worked his way over to it, put it out, and then rebuilt it at a spot so that on their way back the Indians walked off a cliff. He built the fire so that he knew that that would happen!"[3]

Although the tale of killing more than one Indian with a single shot may have been based on a true frontier incident, it may also have been one of Pennsylvania's frontier legends, much like our urban legends of today. A similar story was once circulated about Sam Brady, the famous Indian fighter of the West Branch country, whose hatred of natives was stoked by memories of how his younger brother James had been killed and scalped by a war party near the mouth of Loyalsock Creek in Lycoming County in 1778. The second part of the Coleman account, where the Indians blindly walked off the edge of a cliff while following the glow of their signal fire, has counterparts as well, even as far south as Georgia, and it is not as likely that it is based on true events.

The primeval forests of Pennsylvania, even in the late 1700s, were not easy places to travel through. Careless travelers brave enough to enter them could easily become lost because the woods were "so thick that the tree

---

3. Abraham Lincoln Maurer (born 1872), interviewed May 25, 1974.

trunks almost touch, their height and their matted branches making a dimness cold and fearful, even at noon on the clearest day," wrote David Schoepf in 1783. Adding to the traveler's difficulties besides the many storm-toppled trees and rotting trunks, was the "green and impenetrable bush," described by Schoepf as "difficult to penetrate, even a little way."[4]

Under those conditions it's a wonder that anyone, even the native sons of the forest, could find their way through an early Pennsylvania woods. However, the Indians were too experienced and too attuned to their surroundings to become confused or deterred by nature's obstacles, and even less likely to be taken in by a white man's attempts to confuse them in their native environment.

There are several historical accounts testifying to the Indians' prowess in finding their way through the woods. Using subtle signs like pebbles dislodged by a foot hitting against them, moss on rocks compressed by footfalls, or dry sticks broken by being trodden upon, a native could run circles around a white man when it came to tracking an animal or an enemy. Moravian missionary John Heckewelder, impressed by their uncanny sense of observation, preserved several accounts of their sagacity in his *History of the Indian Nations*. However, the most telling of all Heckewelder's anecdotes is his account of how a settler mistakenly shot an Indian's dog one night. The incident shows just how much advantage natives had over colonists when it came to their powers of observation and their knowledge of the forest.

The canine entered the man's camp one dark night, and the man shot it, mistaking it for a wolf that had raided his store of meat the night before. Able to make its way back to its master's village, the wounded animal caused the owner "much grief and uneasiness" before it expired. Angry at what they thought was an act of malice, the tribesmen confronted the killer, who freely admitted to shooting the dog because he mistook it for a wolf.

Skeptical of the man's statements, an Indian asked him if he really could not tell the difference "between the 'steps' or trampling of a wolf and that of a dog," even on the darkest of nights. When the culprit replied that "no man alive could do that," the band of warriors burst into laughter, amused by "the ignorance of the whites and their want of skill in so plain and common a matter."[5]

4. Stevenson W. Fletcher, *Pennsylvania Agriculture and Country Life, 1640–1840*, 2.

5. Reverend John Heckewelder, *History of the Indian Nations*, 309.

Although the story of how he tricked a band of warriors into walking over a cliff one night is probably just a tale designed to glorify the old man's reputation, Tom Coleman was not alone in his vendetta against the natives. Many hardened frontiersmen harbored the same need for revenge, including one of the harvesters who, with twelve others, was ambushed in the Tuscarora Valley during harvest time in 1763. Found in a mortally wounded condition, it is said that the dying man asked one of the survivors to take his gun and whenever he saw an Indian to kill him with it, vowing that then and only then would he be satisfied.[6]

Of all the frontiersmen whose quest for vengeance against natives seemed unquenchable, there was one who seems to have outdone all the others in his efforts to even the score. Up in Pike County they still talk about Tom Quick, whose entire family was murdered by Indians the family once considered as friendly. In the forty years between that massacre and his own death, it is said that Quick devoted himself to killing natives, logging a total of ninety-nine victims by the time he lay on his death bed. Knowing that he was dying, the dissatisfied backwoodsman begged his friends to bring him his rifle and an Indian so he could "bring his score to an even hundred."[7]

When on his deathbed, Tom Coleman apparently no longer harbored as intense a hatred for the Indians as did Tom Quick. The old frontiersman, who in his later years came to be referred to as "Old Coley" by his former adversaries, passed away quietly at his residence, his thirst for revenge having been quenched at last.

HISTORICAL NOTE: From the time of the first contacts between settlers and the Native American, there was a degree of misunderstanding between the two peoples, which led to mutual distrust. As that distrust led to warfare, both sides of the conflict were guilty of what we would today describe as war crimes. The murder of the younger Coleman brother was one such example of such a crime committed by Native Americans, but colonials were no less guilty of committing war crimes of an equally cruel nature, sometimes even over trivial offenses.

---

6. C. Hale Sipe, *The Indian Chiefs of Pennsylvania*, 379.

7. Grant N. Sassaman, editor, *Pennsylvania, a Guide to the Keystone State*, 356.

As one historian has confirmed, "The white man did not understand his red neighbor and was always suspicious of him." As an example, that same historian goes on to say, "It was not the Indian's custom to knock on the door of a neighbor's house before entering and wait to be invited in. Instead, he just opened the door and walked in."[8]

The Indians were just as communal about sharing food, considering it to be common property, and so by nature "felt he had a perfect right to food wherever he found it." It was a custom the settlers had trouble understanding, much less tolerating, and it proved to be unbearable in the case of one Potter County pioneer family during the times of the first settlement in that remote wilderness.

The family was somewhat used to the repeated visits of their native neighbors, which usually entailed requests for food. The family would always honor the requests without complaint, but one day when the husband was away, one warrior, meaning no disrespect nor harm, managed to change that attitude. Noticing a pot of steaming stew hanging on the fireplace crane, the hungry man dipped his excessively dirty hands into the pot and helped himself. This brazen act upset the pioneer housewife so much that she vented about it to her husband when he returned, complaining in no uncertain terms about how it had ruined her stew. Equally upset over what he too considered an intolerable violation of their privacy, he "took out after the Indian and in due time returned with nothing to say. The Indian never came back."[9]

The implication here being that he found the Indian and exacted a vengeful and odious punishment which hardly matched the offense in question. Acts like this were black marks against early Pennsylvania pioneers, whose work ethic was exemplary and whose moral conduct was usually admirable.

NOTE ON SPANGLER'S FORT OR BLOCKHOUSE: Built sometime before 1800 by John Christopher Spangler to protect his family from attacks, this historic building stood as a unique reminder of Pennsylvania's frontier days until a new owner of the property had it bulldozed down in 1967, despite the chagrin and efforts of locals and of state historians to save it.

---

8. Arch P. Akeley, "Indians in Potter County," *Historical Sketches of Potter County*, 1.
9. Ibid.

Spangler's Fort or Blockhouse (Centre County). Photo and information courtesy of Vonnie Henninger, direct descendant of John Spangler. Built sometime before 1800 by John Christopher Spangler to protect his family from Indian attacks, this historic building stood as a unique reminder of Pennsylvania's frontier days until a new owner of the property had it bulldozed down in 1967, despite the chagrin and efforts of locals and of state historians to save it.

The Rev. J. J. Weaver of Rebersburg described Spangler's Fort in the following way in a newspaper article he wrote sometime in the 1930s:

There still remains the Block House on the farm now owned by Mr. O. F. Stover, 2 miles east of Rebersburg. It is still in a fine state of preservation . . . The old fort was erected before the year 1800 on land owned by Christopher Spangler, who acquired this land with others from various individuals . . . Now as to the old Block House or fort, for such it was, erected by presumably Christopher Spangler, for protection against marauding bands of Indians, who at that time were mostly in the western part of Pennsylvania but who made incursions to the central and eastern portions of the state to steal if they so willed to murder some unsuspecting whites . . . It is built of mountain sandstone with the following dimensions: 10 ft. wide x 13 ft. long, 10 ft. high, walls 2 ft. 4 in. thick. There are two floors, both with very low ceilings. On the upper floor there are 7 loopholes through which rifles could be used against an enemy. 2 loopholes on each of the east, west, and southern walls, and one that faces the north. On the outer edge these loopholes or slits in the wall are filled in by placing small stones therein, so the old building could be used as a smoke house to smoke meat. There are two heavy doors on the western side, for this faced the original house, which stood just a few feet south of the present large stone house erected in 1805. A building of the proportions of this Block House would scarcely give protection, but to one family, for which it was unquestionably erected. This writer has visited many old fort sites and some buildings that were used as forts in Indian days, but none are so well preserved as the little Spangler Block House.

Johnathan Spangler Sr. (1766–1855). Son of Christopher Spangler, he more than likely helped his father build the Spangler Blockhouse.

CHAPTER 7

KINGS OF THE HILLS

Positioned at the top of nature's food chain, Pennsylvania mountain lions, also referred to as panthers or painters by the state's earliest hunters, were long considered kings of all the hills, valleys, hollows, and forests they surveyed. Even though the animals were fond of haunting the wildest glens and the most inaccessible and untamed parts of the forest, panthers were still numerous enough in those early days that pioneer families had to always be on their guard. But eventually, through untiring merciless efforts, those settlers gained the upper hand and pushed the beasts further and further westward, until there were only a few remote valleys and glens where the animals could maintain a presence in their original domain.

As time went on, even those few strongholds in Penn's Woods dwindled, and panthers were less frequently encountered here, seemingly disappearing altogether in the last two decades following the end of the Civil War. The presumption that the animal could then be considered extinct in Pennsylvania seems to have been a little like the erroneous report announcing the death of author Mark Twain. The announcement was, said the much-loved and very much alive humorist, "greatly exaggerated."

Stories of panther sightings in the Pennsylvania wilds, and even of attacks on humans, continued through the 1890s, and sightings, some believe, continue until the present day. Such reports, from the oldest to even the more recent ones, catch peoples' attention, and so are likely to be remembered by those who hear them.

It is perhaps for this reason that just thirty years ago I could still find senior citizens who would gladly relate to me tales they had heard about panther encounters that occurred during the beast's twilight days in Pennsylvania; stories remembered by those who were born during that twilight time and who had heard the tales from those who lived them. Since the purpose of my *Pennsylvania Fireside Tales* books is to preserve these types of stories for posterity, I would be remiss if I did not include as many as I can of the more interesting panther tales I've collected over the years, these throwbacks to another age, in my writings.

Some of these anecdotes have already been preserved in the first four volumes of this series, but there are others in my files that seemed as though they would give me no rest until they appeared on the printed page. Not one to keep a good story down, I've dedicated this chapter to another: that chapter in Pennsylvania's history that might be correctly called the swan song of the panther.

On the pages that follow are a few of those swan songs; tales from the time period of 1860 to 1900 when the mountain lion was making its last desperate attempts to maintain its position as king of the Pennsylvania forests. However, the story of that struggle does not encompass just the last half of the nineteenth century. In fact, it began when the first settlers entered lion country.

Included in the historical annals of Clinton County is an early narrative which shows just how hopeless the panther's struggle was in the contest between man and beast. It is an account typical of many others, recalling that even the boldest panthers were no match for a brave pioneer determined to protect his livestock.

Early records show that when Clinton County's Sugar Valley was first settled during the 1820s and 1830s, one of the earliest pioneers there was Henry Barner. Resourceful and hard-working, Barner chose to build his homestead on the mountains north of present day Logansville, a choice he was later to regret when he realized that not only had he settled in a place where the soil was not the best for farming, but that he had also trespassed onto territory that the local panthers claimed as their exclusive fiefdom.

Like many of his fellow settlers, Barner raised some chickens and pigs to supplement his larder, keeping his poultry in a chicken coop and his hogs in a pen. Although the crowing of roosters and the squealing of pigs are everyday sounds that anyone who raises them becomes accustomed to, Barner noticed one day that his pigs were squealing more than usual.

When he went to investigate, he was amazed to see a huge painter trying to get one of his pigs through a hole in the pigpen's fence. After going back for his gun, the determined pioneer returned to the site and shot the panther just as it was ready to pounce upon him.

The unlucky panther proved to be a monster, measuring over eleven feet long from the tip of its nose to the tip of its tail, and was said to be the largest ever seen in the region. Barner didn't seem to be particularly impressed with his trophy, leaving it in his front yard to slowly decompose.

The news of this unusual trophy rapidly spread to nearby settlements and attracted many curious mountain folks who came by just to get a firsthand look at the formidable beast that had recently been a denizen of the nearby woods. Among those visitors was Dr. Casper Wistar, Professor of Anatomy at the University of Pennsylvania, and owner of several thousand acres in Sugar Valley.

After hearing about the Barner panther on one of his occasional visits to his holdings in the valley, Dr. Wistar had his servant hitch the horses to his wagon and take him to the Barner cabin. Upon their arrival the men could see the rotting panther lying in Barner's front yard. Spurred on by his scientific curiosity and seemingly indifferent to the condition of the specimen, Dr. Wistar ordered the servant to put the beast's head in the carriage, saying it would be interesting to take it back to Philadelphia where it could be dissected and studied. The reluctant assistant retrieved the head, but as he was carrying the grinning skull back to the carriage, he was overheard muttering to himself, "Bad smell! Bad smell!"[1]

Henry Barner, and the other old-time "hill hawks" who shared the mountains with the big cats they often referred to as painters, could have told Dr. Wistar's valet that it was not usually an offensive odor that revealed the presence of these intimidating animals. Most of the time, they would have averred, the beasts were heard before they were close enough to be seen, their characteristic screams sometimes carrying for over a half mile or more when conditions were just right.

It was a sound of the wild that often struck as much fear into the heart of a solitary traveler as did the howls of a wolf pack in full cry. "When the

---

1. John Blair Linn, *History of Centre and Clinton Counties, Pennsylvania*, 614.

panther made known his presence," recalled an early Potter County settler, "it was a blood-curdling cry, which resembled the shrill shriek of a women in deadly peril!"[2]

When collecting tales and anecdotes for my books, I was surprised to find that, even as late as the first year of the twenty-first century, there were still some old-time Pennsylvania mountaineers who either recalled hearing the painter's cry themselves or who, in their younger days, had descriptions of it passed on to them by others who had heard it years before. Without fail, they all seemed to agree that the sounds were not pleasant ones, even though they sometimes reminded them of something more innocent and defenseless.

Old-time lumberman Royal Kline, born in 1901, was one of those who had heard the painter's cry himself. Some ninety years later he could still remember it just as clearly as it sounded that night in 1910 when it caught the attention of the Kline family, whose homestead sat in the deep woods of California Hollow; near the small Blair County village of Bald Eagle, and much further back on the Allegheny Mountain than the houses that sit in the same hollow today.

"It was right close to our home, and the dogs raised the devil that night!" recalled the old man, who was one year short of the century mark when we talked to him in January of 2000. "The foxhounds carried on terrible," explained Mr. Kline when asked to describe the cries of the animal that sent the dogs into a frenzy on that particular evening. "Oh, it would squall and squall," he continued, "and then it would go 'ue!, ue!, ue!'" [like the letters ue sound when the word glue is spoken].

The unexpected ending to the panther's terrible serenade was the most surprising thing about it. It was in stark contrast to the first part of its unwelcome song and, said Mr. Kline, it sounded "just like when a baby 'schnitzes'."[3]

Harvey Lindthurst, another old-time lumberman who worked on the tram railway that ran from Milroy in Mifflin County back into the wildest parts of the Seven Mountains country during the 1880s, often told his family how he would hear panthers calling when he rode the "dinky" back at night. The cries, he would recall, sounded to him "just like a baby."[4]

2. J. H. Beers & Co., *History of the Counties of McKean, Elk, Cameron, and Potter, Pennsylvania, Volume II*, 998.

3. Royal Kline (born July 7, 1901), recorded January 2, 2000.

4. Clarence Lindthurst (born 1907), interviewed December 17, 1986.

Ralph Stamm, born in 1914, also remembered similar sounds he heard in the autumn of 1924 when his family moved from their farm over in the Loop, near the little village of Colyer in Centre County, to a new farm over the Allegheny mountains north of the village of Unionville in that same county.

Most people in those days didn't have trucks to transport their belongings or their cattle when they had, in the vernacular of the times, a flittin'. Whenever a family moved to a new farm in those horse-and-buggy days, they carried their belongings in wagons, and they would drive their cows overland, much like the huge cattle drives of the Old West and a sight still remembered by those who grew up in rural Pennsylvania during the 1920s.

The Stamm family's flitting was typical of others in those days, with their household goods and farm tools loaded in horse-drawn wagons following behind a herd of slow-moving cattle. It was a long, hard, trip compared to today, with no paved highways to smooth the ride, and the Stamms were jostled about as they traveled over a bumpy and dusty old wagon road out of the Loop.

Eventually, during the course of their flitting, the Stamms crossed over present-day State Penitentiary grounds, intending to pass through Buffalo Run Valley, cross over the Bald Eagle Mountain, and then cross the mountains above Unionville by following the dizzying heights of the old Rattlesnake Pike down into the next valley, where they would settle into their new homestead.

It was raining hard the night the Stamm's caravan reached the Buffalo Run Church, and here they stopped, intending to wait out the storm and spend the night in their wagon. This was where they would have slept, had a Good Samaritan not told them they could spend the night in the church if they so desired. It was a night that the Stamm's son Ralph fondly remembered in his later years, but the thing about the flitting that left the greatest impression on the young lad were the frightening noises he and his family heard after dark.

Every night of the Stamms' journey over the Bald Eagle Mountain and along the Rattlesnake Pike, sharp piercing cries would come from somewhere on the mountaintops and would sometimes be repeated from uninviting pitch-dark hollows down below. As the caterwauling continued, the sounds seemed magnified by echoes that came from nearby peaks, and Ralph's father made a point of drawing his young son to his side to comfort him.

The nocturnal sounds, he explained, came from what he thought were panthers calling to one another in the darkness. No matter how frightful the sounds, he cautioned his intimidated youngster, he must not be afraid. A person's fear, he said, had a unique odor that masked the panthers' ability to smell men, but as long as the beasts scented people, they would not have the courage to attack them or their livestock.

The Stamms were never bothered by the menacing beasts that Mr. Stamm thought were mountain lions, nor were their cattle, but the noise the panthers made left an indelible impression on Ralph Stamm's memory. The unusual sounds, he recalled, were "Just like a young deer calling its mother, baby-like sounds."[5]

In 1925, Clinton County farm boys Casper and Joe Peters were shocking corn by hand on the family farm located in one of the valleys lying along the Tangascootack Mountain, when they heard a panther's cry. "It squalled awful, and you could hear it a mile away! It's enough to make the chills go up your back," recalled the old man in 2002 when describing the animal's cries to us and explaining that the calls were, in his words, "unusual."

"It wasn't a wildcat," he claimed, explaining that the squalls of a wildcat "sound more like a cat," while these calls had an underlying tone that had a softer quality to it. "Something between a baby's cries and a cat," was the way he put it, when attempting to tell us what he had heard on that particular afternoon some seventy-seven years ago.[6]

Although the panther's song may have a baby-like quality to it, it was the full-throated roar of the beast that most often caught the attention of those who lived during the days when the animals were not as scarce as they appear to be today. That awful cry set peoples' nerves on edge, especially if they heard it when a loved one was still out in the fields alone as darkness approached, or when a family member was walking back home after visiting a neighbor several miles down the valley. It was a painter's wail just like this that alarmed Sam Ertel's wife and daughter one evening

---

5. Ralph Stamm (born 1914), interviewed March 1, 1985.
6. Casper Peters (born 1908), recorded May 21, 2002.

Casper Peters. In 1925 he heard the "painters" cry in Clinton County.

during the 1860s, when he was a little late in returning from a day of butchering at his brother-in-law's farm in Centre County.

"I wanta tell you a story. It's just interesting," began Sam Ertel's granddaughter. Her tale was one she had heard from her mother, who had been there the night the panther passed through their little valley.

Sam Ertel had spent that entire day helping George Gentzel butcher at his Georges Valley farm "down in the hollow below the church." He had not yet returned home when his wife and daughter heard blood-curdling screams from something that was traveling along the crest of the mountain back of their home. "Oh, she said it hollered something terrific," explained our storyteller, recalling what her mother had described to her. "They thought it was a panther," she went on. "They didn't know, and they didn't see it, but she said it hollered so! She said she set and pulled her feet up under her, under the chair. You know how a kid will do."

"Grandma was scared too. She was afraid that this thing would smell the blood that was probably on Grandpa's clothes and meet him on the road! He got home all right, but Grandma was worried. They say that's the last time they heard panthers around here. They didn't know, but they thought sure that's what it was because the way it hollered. Oh, she said it made awful!"[7]

---

7. Mrs. Randall Steiger (born 1903), recorded May 4, 1988.

Samuel Ertle. Born in 1837, he had a
number of close-calls with mountain lions
in his day. (Photo courtesy of Robert Steiger)

Mrs. Mary A. (Minich) Ertle. Born in
1835, she married Samuel Ertle in 1859.
(Photo courtesy of Robert Steiger)

Ellen and Minnie Crater would argue, were they still alive, that the Ertel panther was not the last one whose frightful cries broke the silence of these hills on an otherwise peaceful night. They would, no doubt, tell of the panther they heard in the valley next to Georges Valley one evening as they made their way home through the mountains after attending a young people's gathering at their church.

There was a big revival meeting at the mountain church in Lingle Valley that night. It was a social event just for the younger generations, and so most of the attendees had tramped along rocky wagon roads or hiked along narrow mountain trails to get there. Young people from nearby Georges, Decker, and Kohler Valleys could have probably been seen there that night, but the Crater girls had a much shorter walk since their home in the Zerby Gap was only a half mile from the church. Perhaps it was because it was such a short trip that they made it alone, leaving their widowed mother behind as they eagerly went out the front door and headed for the evening's activities.

In those days, revival meetings were one of the social events of the times, and everyone that had come to the mountain church on this evening probably talked and laughed outside until it was time for the service to begin.

Amanda C. Ertle. Born in 1859, she was the daughter of Samuel and Mary Ertle and wife of John W. Gobble. See the chapter titled "Sam Ertle's Panthers" in Pennsylvania Fireside Tales Volume 1 *for a panther story about one of her father's panther encounters that chilled her to the bone. Photo courtesy of Robert Steiger)*

Once inside, the attendees no doubt became more solemn and reserved as they sang revival meeting hymns and listened to the preacher's sermon.

Interesting and invigorating as the proceedings might have been, young minds would tend to wander to outside concerns and thoughts as the evening wore on, but if they did not, they most certainly would have done so when the service was interrupted several times by noises that sounded like loud screams, coming down off a nearby mountaintop.

Eventually the noises stopped and were not repeated again, and no one seemed concerned enough to think twice about the walk back through the mountains to their homes in the wild hollows and sequestered clearings of the deep woods. Probably none of those at the church that night had ever heard a wild animal that sounded like this one; one whose caterwauls were loud enough and unusual enough to cause the singing to stop and heads to turn at the revival service.

It had perhaps been twenty or thirty years since the Ertels had heard similar cries over in Georges Valley, and so the noise probably was not

The Brush Panther. One of the last native mountain lions killed in Pennsylvania was shot up in the northeastern section of Susquehanna County by Samuel Brush about 1857. Now this last "Nittany Lion" sits peacefully at rest behind a glass display window just inside the front entrance to Pattee Library at Penn State's University Park Campus, in Centre County – just recently moved to the Sports Museum at the football stadium.

taken as seriously as it should have been by the young revivalists and their minister. They would not have realized the danger that was lurking along the roads and trails that they would all have to travel on that night.

After the revival service ended, the attendees went their separate ways; each to his home in the hills. For most the trip was uneventful, and the sight of the warm glow of lanterns in the windows of their parents' houses was a pleasant way to end their evening. To Minnie and Ellen Crater, however, the trip home was far from uneventful, and the soft yellow color of lantern lights in their mother's windows turned out to be a beacon of refuge.

Shortly after they began their short walk back home the Crater girls once again heard the strange squalls that had interrupted the church service that evening. Walking a little faster, the girls moved on, but eventually they realized that the sounds were getting closer and closer, and that whatever was making the weird cries was following them home.

By the time the badly frightened girls finally made it back and were safely inside, the animal was at the barn. As the girls and their mother looked at it from the safety of the house, they could see it clearly in the moonlight. It was, said their mother, the animal the old timers once called a "painter." With a look that might have been one of disdain, the beast gave one last defiant cry and then disappeared. It was probably the last of its kind ever seen in the northern Seven Mountains again.[8]

NOTE: The Crater homestead is used as a hunting camp today, but the little church where the revival meeting was held no longer exists. It was truly a little brown church in the wildwood; but was usually referred to as the mountain church by its parishioners. Its cemetery is still used for interments and is kept in good condition by dedicated caretakers.

---

8. Clarence Musser (born 1884), interviewed August 28, 1971, and November 12, 1971.

CHAPTER 8

STASHING IT AWAY

Based on historical accounts and on the snippets of oral history that have come down to us, it seems that outlaw gangs were as common in Pennsylvania at one time as they were in the wild and wooly American West. Although none of these Pennsylvania desperados became as infamous as some of their western counterparts did, Jesse James and his gang being one of the best-known examples of this western breed; bad men of the Keystone State were just as determined to accomplish their ends as were the outlaws of the Old West.

Starting at about the time of the Revolutionary War and up until the end of the Civil War, there were numerous gangs in various parts of the state that preyed upon the unsuspecting and the vulnerable. Some of these bands of ruffians achieved higher levels of notoriety than others, but even among this group the Doanes of southeastern Pennsylvania seemed to be in a category of their own.

One of the most notorious outlaw gangs in Pennsylvania at one time, the Doane bunch consisted of men whose backgrounds were not consistent with that calling. Moses Doane and his brothers were Quakers, that religious sect usually known for their love of peace and their kindness toward others, but rather than following the path of their brethren, the Doanes instead chose to become common thieves.

However, the brothers were also endowed with remarkable athletic abilities, which they were not afraid to use to impress others, a trait that also seems to be at odds with a profession that requires those who pursue it

A treasure chest filled with glowing gold coins. Every treasure-hunter's dream and an artist's conception of what it might look like.

to remain out of the public view most of the time. But it seems the brothers liked to show off more than lay low, at least according to one account from Lancaster County.

"In Lancaster they had some shindig goin' and the guy jumped over the Conestoga wagon," explained an older resident of the Pennsylvania Dutch country one day, when he was telling us about the infamous brothers. "And they said, 'My God, what a feat!' you know. And somebody said, 'It either has to be the devil or one of the Doanes!'"[1]

There were those who probably thought the Black Prince was indeed in league with the Doanes at the height of their career. This occurred, some would argue, during the most trying days of the Revolutionary War, when the brothers found that stealing horses and cattle from their neighbors and selling them to the British troops in Philadelphia was a profitable business. But even reaching this level of villainy didn't seem to satisfy the Doanes, and eventually the honest citizens of Bucks, Montgomery, and Berks Counties became victims of the brothers' crime wave as well.

The hard-pressed citizens of these same counties were subjected to similar trials some seventy-five years later, when Abe Buzzard and his gang plagued the populace of the Blue Mountains during the Civil War. Like the Doanes, the Buzzards seem to have little compassion for those they robbed,

---

1. L. W. Bumbaugh (born 1910), interviewed August 27, 1972, recorded August 22, 1989.

at least according to one folktale that the older folks of the Blue Mountain country could still recall, over one-hundred years after the Buzzard Gang had faded into oblivion, their infamy preserved only in the minds of those who had heard about them from the gang's victims.

"They used to put girls out when they were twelve or fourteen years old," recalled the Berks Countian whose grandmother was one of those young ladies; girls whose parents, like other parents who were hard-pressed for cash in those days, had them join the work force at a young age so they could earn extra money for their families.

"She told me they used to have these gangs go around and rob, you know. Some of them took it from the rich and gave it to the poor. Well, down here, right here in what's called Niantic, down here on the other side of the bridge at Shultz's Mill, she was working there one time when she was young when this gang, the Buzzard Gang, they called them, Buzzards, came to rob.

"And they came in the house, you know, and the woman, Mrs. Shultz, wanted to save some of the stuff, and throw it out the window upstairs. And one of the guys seen it. He says, 'There's no use of doing that, because there's just as many of us outside as there is inside.'"[2]

Over the years other counties in Pennsylvania were not lucky enough to be exempted from the ravages of outlaw gangs either. The Gap Gang of Lancaster, York, and Chester Counties were notorious hold-up men and counterfeiters in that region. Further west, over in Butler County, a group of cattle and horse thieves known as the Stone House Gang would steal horses and cattle from the drovers on the Pittsburgh-Franklin and Butler-Mercer turnpikes.

Other gangs throughout the state must have conducted their dirty business in anonymity, with only placenames, in some cases, preserving a record of their deeds; the Robbers Cave near Pleasant Unity in Westmoreland County being one such example. There were, on the other hand, sections of the state that seem to have had more than their share of the criminal element, a condition that was particularly true during the formative years of the country.

One notable locale like this was situated in that part of York County which was once claimed by both Maryland and Pennsylvania. Legal

---

2. Ibid.

jurisdictions and boundaries were ill-defined at this time because of a territorial dispute over the southern part of York County, and since no one seemed certain who had legal authority in the area, the end result was ineffective or reduced law enforcement.

Word about this seemingly lawless area was soon widely circulated among the criminal element, which for some reason considered the area around present-day Hanover, York County, rather than surrounding areas, to be the best haven from both Pennsylvania and Maryland lawmen. Soon the locals nicknamed the notorious section "Rogues' Rest," a name which perhaps eventually helped to convince the two states to settle their territorial differences so they could deal with this den of thieves once and for all.

Among the worst of the worst in the annals of Pennsylvania's criminal groups were those rogues from Philadelphia known as the Schuylkill Rangers. These bold miscreants made a career of preying upon the canal boats of the coal region's Schuylkill Canal, and they eventually became so successful and so imperious, that they even tried to attack whole towns.

Schuylkill Haven and Pottsville were two such targets, but here the Rangers were thwarted by groups of well-armed citizens who had no intention of letting the blackguards carry out their plans. The Rangers were most successful when they used guerilla tactics, one of which was to hide on one of the many bridges over the canal and to drop onto canal boats when the boats were passing underneath. It was a tactic that was used often enough that at least one of the canal boatmen eventually decided to retaliate.

The story of how the tough old canal boat captain exacted his revenge, in one of the decades immediately preceding the Civil War, was once a popular tale in Dauphin and Cumberland Counties. Here, on the canal between Union Deposit and Pine Grove Furnace, the scruffy navigator, accompanied by his faithful dog, made regular trips, hauling coal from one town to the other.

All his voyages were made during daylight hours, and so he felt fairly secure, knowing that the Schuylkill Rangers couldn't surprise him under cover of darkness. But one sunlit day the captain let down his guard and failed to notice several of the Rangers hiding on a bridge just ahead. As the canal boat passed underneath, the robbers jumped from their hiding places and landed upon the captain. The wily navigator, although surprised, was not overcome by his assailants and managed to get his hands on two flint-lock muskets he had kept handy for use in just this situation.

"He unloaded on 'em and got two of 'em," explained the old gentle-man who was recalling the incident for us, and who claimed it was a true story he had once read about.

The third mugger was luckier. After using his flintlocks to kill two of the three thugs, the captain grabbed an axe and took off after the third man, chasing him through a nearby woods but never quite getting close enough to administer his coup de grace. When local authorities found out about the incident they took the feisty captain to court, where a judge put him in prison for twenty-four hours. It must have perplexed the defendant a bit, since to him it was a clear-cut case of self-defense. However, the judge's explanation probably didn't make the convicted man feel any better about the sentence meted out to him. "He asked the judge why he put him in prison," noted our storyteller, "and the judge said, 'Because you didn't get the other one!'[3]

Other victims of gang robberies would have applauded the judge's sentiments. Given the prevalence and boldness of thieves in those early days, it's not hard to understand why people would often prefer to put their valuables and their money in secret hiding places rather than entrust them to someone else. To many it probably seemed that no house or no bank was safe enough, and for those folks it seemed safer to stash their valuables in their own homes or to bury money somewhere on their property.

"I'd like to know how much money's buried in the mountains yet, at some of these old places," mused another gentleman who was telling us about one such house. "I know a fella who had money stashed all over, and I guess he had some buried in the garden. Nobody's found it yet. His wife even didn't know where it was. Grey Harper—he was always that poor, he couldn't buy matches to light his own pipe. He was that poor, and yet he had all kinds of money. He had it all over the house—hid under the rugs and hid every place else. Never had no money!" The old gentlemen then

3. George Korson, *Pennsylvania Songs and Legends*, 262, 272, 276; James Stephens (born 1924), recorded April 13, 1989 and December 23, 1989.

leaned back and lit up his own pipe, almost as an act of contempt for the miser he had just described to us.[4]

Other people apparently wanted to make it even more difficult for others to find their cash, and according to an older resident of Berks County, the good citizens of Montgomery and Berks found a particularly unique way of hiding theirs. "The people used to throw their money down in the well. Now, I did hear over near Pottstown there was a guy died, and they said he had throwed his money down in the well, and that they pumped the well out and got it out. There's a lot of places I should check out. There's places burnt down up in the Furnace Hills near Landis Store where they were making moonshine. That's why the place burned down; it blew up. But wells like that, I wonder if there are; or maybe they buried [their money]. I know of other places up in the hills where there used to be old houses. Way up in the Forgedale Hills you can still see a farm where a stone fence was around the buildings, you know. I should go check," said the old Dutchman, contemplating his chances of finding a long-forgotten fortune that had once been stashed away so that it would be safe from thieves.[5]

Over in England it was once thought that one way to keep a home safe was to sacrifice an animal and bury it under the foundation when the house was being built. The animals' ghost, it was believed, would "guard the building against evil influences."[6]

Likewise in this country, in situations where a house was left vacant because a family succumbed to a virulent tuberculosis or flu epidemic, or some other plague, there was often speculation about how well the family had guarded their valuables. In these cases, it was especially common for rumors to circulate about the treasure that was buried somewhere on those premises.

Similar tales like this once were widely circulated about General Philip Benner's mansion in Centre County. Benner, a veteran of the Revolutionary War, became a successful ironmaster in Centre County after the war. His Rock Iron Works were located on ground now owned by the Rockview Correctional Institution near State College. The stately mansion that

---

4. Wilbur Auman (born 1915), recorded November 19, 1988.

5. L. W. Bumbaugh (born 1910), interviewed August 27, 1972, recorded August 22, 1989.

6. H. H. Hain, *History of Perry County, Pennsylvania*, 552.

Beware the frenzy of the fairy ring! Artist's illustration of a man being saved from certain death by being pulled from a fairy circle and its fairies. Illustration from British Goblins Welsh Folk-lore, Fairy Mythology, Legends and Traditions *by Wirt Sikes, published in London, 1880.*

Benner built here for his family after he became a successful ironmaster was evidence of his wealth, but, like many such places, the Benner mansion fell into disrepair after the General's death.

Finally, there came a time when no one lived in the place at all, and the house eventually fell into total ruin. However, people still came to the place, lured there by the tales of the money the General had buried in the cellar floor. Evidence of the treasure seekers' efforts could once be seen in the form of many holes dug down into the spot where the cellar floor had been.

The possibility of buried treasure has always been a strong lure to many folks, and greed tends to warp even honest men's minds, sometimes turning them into thieves. At least, if the story is a true account, which seems to be what happened near the little Centre County town of Woodward one time.

Here, near this quaint mountain village, it was once believed that the Eby family had hidden gold all over their farm. However, a neighbor supposedly found out where it was, so the story goes; and he stole it, burying most of it in his own hiding place. Somehow the authorities linked him to the crime and had enough evidence to send him to jail. During his stay in prison the thief was visited by one of the "upstanding" citizens of Woodward, who told him he "should have someone take care of his money for him."

At first the robber didn't want any part of this scheme, but eventually was persuaded to reveal the location of a tree under which he had buried a jar of gold coins. After the thief had finally served his time in jail, he went to look for his jar. It was no longer there, but it is said that his "mentor" lived very prosperously; proving once again the old adage that there is no honor among thieves.[7]

---

7. Wilbur Auman (born 1915), recorded November 19, 1988.

CHAPTER 9

A WITCH'S BREW

"Art thou a witch?" asked William Penn when Margaret Mattson was brought before him and other members of the Provincial Council in 1683. Accused of bewitching her neighbors' cattle and causing them to die, the old woman was confused and intimidated by the proceedings.

"Hast though ridden through the air on a broomstick?" continued Penn, who was sitting as magistrate of the Council. When the addled matron replied that she had indeed done so, Penn, in a display of his good common sense and compassion for his fellow man, noted that it was her privilege to do so, as he "knew of no law against it."[1] Upon his recommendation, the jurors found the frightened woman "Guilty of having the common fame of a witch, but not Guilty in the manner and forme as she stands indicted." Without further deliberation they released the hex under recognizance of her husband, who paid a fine of fifty pounds for his wife's misdemeanor.[2]

During that early colonial period in the state's history there were numerous old women who had the common fame of being a witch. It was not an uncommon belief in those days that personal misfortune could be blamed upon witches and that they could do many marvelous things, like riding on a broomstick. However, what is really remarkable about these beliefs today is how long it took for them to die. As noted in some of the previous stories in my *Pennsylvania Fireside Tales* volumes, even as late as

---

1. J. C. Furnas, *The Americans, A Social History of the United States 1587–1914*, 78.
2. Frederic A. Godcharles, *Daily Stories of Pennsylvania*, 150.

the 1970s I could still find people who harbored similar beliefs; the very same ideas that were held by their colonial ancestors two-hundred years earlier.

Although stories of witches, and the supernatural things they could do, seem to have been limited only by peoples' imaginations, there were always some recurrent themes that underpinned those stories; common beliefs that were held by all who accepted witch tales as accounts of factual episodes. Included in these basic tenets was the idea that witches could use broomsticks as a method of flying through the air, but there were many others as well.

After thirty years of collecting the oral history and legendary lore of Pennsylvania, I've ended up with a considerable number of hex tales; a bewitching collection of anecdotes which incorporate in one way or another all the basic superstitions that comprise the witch genre. This chapter contains some of those tales, which, I think, include some of the best I've been able to collect over the years. The fact that I was still able to collect them in the last quarter of the twentieth century indicates to me that, since they survived for fifty years or more, they were among the most popular ones of their day.

The tales that are recorded here are not extracts from earlier-day texts, but are accounts passed on to me by people who I've talked to throughout the Commonwealth. Many of those who related the episodes had heard them from older folks who implicitly believed in their truth, but most of those who entertained me with the stories no longer believed that the supernatural parts of the accounts could be true.

However, some of my storytellers did still believe that such accounts were completely factual; did think that witches could once wring milk from towels, turn into black cats, cast horrible spells upon both people and animals alike or render them immobile, and hear anything anyone was saying about them on certain days of the year (unless the person speaking was under a roof!)

A typical account about a witch milking a towel was once a popular topic of conversation in and around the small village of Beaver Dam in Centre County (see the chapter entitled "The Beaver Dam Witch" in volume IV of the author's *Pennsylvania Fireside Tales* series), but there were other reputed

Hexerei Over the Rhine. This witch on her broomstick can be seen inside a museum display window in the small village of Rudesheim, along the Rhine River in Germany. The little museum contains many fascinating artifacts of that period of time when Europeans believed that witchcraft and witches were more powerful than the forces of nature itself. Today we consider such beliefs to be merely quaint ideas from ages past, but centuries ago people believed that witches having powers like this one actually existed and were powers to be reckoned with.

witches in that same county, who people thought could do the very same thing. Over in Madisonburg and in the surrounding countryside, locals once believed that Betsy Zettle had the power to get milk from a towel, while down in Milllheim there were those who claimed to have actually seen Fayette Wingard milking a towel on numerous occasions.

The folks in Millheim were not surprised to hear such things about their resident witch. Here it was widely accepted that the old hex got great delight in not only milking towels but also in exercising her powers in other ways as well. She could, it was believed, cast her spells from a distance, causing people to lose sleep at night by putting lumps in their feather ticks or by knotting the horsehairs in their pillows.

Although it's not known today how many of these kinds of accusations got back to the reputed witch, most women in those times would probably

Hexerei Over the Rhine - Closeup of the witch. This unique museum had some graphic displays inside as well, revealing the many facets of the witchcraft scare all over Europe. The cruel punishments almost made our Salem witchcraft trials look tame in comparison!

have been insulted by this kind of slander. However, during that same time period there was at least one woman in that same valley who seemed to delight in such notoriety.

Sadie Dietzel liked to flaunt her powers, or so it appeared to those who believed that the old woman could get milk from an ordinary bath or dish towel. Sadie lived along the foot of Tussey Mountain in the western end of Penn's Valley in Centre County, near the small village of Tusseyville, during the 1920s. Although neighborly in some ways, she was held in high disregard by some of her neighbors because they believed that whenever their cows wouldn't produce milk, Sadie was the cause.

"Here comes Sadie for milk," was often the remark that was made when someone spotted the old woman coming down the road carrying her bucket in one hand and twirling a towel in the other. On these excursions Sadie made a point of walking by her neighbors' barns, and many were the agriculturalists who were convinced that their cows would soon go dry when they saw Sadie pass by.

Sadie, they believed, was capable of somehow drawing their cows' milk into her towel as she nonchalantly strolled along while carrying out her strange performance. After making her rounds, the supposed hex could be seen heading home, bucket in hand and her towel over her arm.

There were those who were mildly amused by the eccentric old lady's behavior; but others thought that once she was inside her house she could finish her task, get the milk she had gone to collect. This she did, claimed those who believed in her powers, by using the same towel that she twirled in the air as she took her walks through the morning mist.

Her procedure for getting the milk in this supernatural way, said the believers, was to first roll up the towel and hang it over the arm of a chair. Although no one could claim to have seen these things first-hand and know for sure what happened next, the common belief was that once the towel was in place Sadie would repeat a mysterious incantation over it and then proceed to milk it.

This she did by squeezing and pulling on the ends of the towel, just as though she were milking a live cow. If anyone had the nerve to peek in her window while she was doing her milking, claimed the pundits who knew about such things, they would see streams of creamy white liquid squirting from the ends of Sadie's towel. It was, said the same authorities, the witch's way of getting her milk for free and with the least amount of trouble, even though it was at her neighbors' expense.[3]

It would have taken extraordinary powers of persuasion to convince The Tussey Mountain farmers that they were wrong about Sadie Dietzel's ability to steal their cows' milk by simply using a towel. Superstitions about

---

3. Paul Zerby (born March 20, 1919), recorded August 6, 2000.

witchcraft were still prevalent among Pennsylvania's agricultural popula-
tions even at that late day, but these were ideas that had deep roots. Such
beliefs, including the notion that witches could milk towels, had been
instilled in generation after generation of descendants of the state's earliest
settlers, whose forebears had indoctrinated the same beliefs in them.

Pioneer families who settled in southwestern Pennsylvania in the 1700s
were no doubt representative of the state's other pioneer families at that
time, as far as the superstitions they held, and among those superstitions
was the idea that witches could use towels to steal milk from their neighbors' cows. Here it was believed that the witch didn't even have to pass by
a farmer's barnyard to draw his cows' milk into her towel.

"Fixing a new pin in a new towel for each cow intended to be milked,"
was the witch's preferred approach in this part of the state. After that, the
procedure was pretty much the same as Sadie Dietzel's, except here it was
thought that the witch hung the towel over her door before milking it in
the "manner of milking a cow."[4]

Despite the many believers at that time, there were skeptics who scoffed
at the idea that witches could use black magic to steal a cow's milk. Accusations to this effect arose, noted one such skeptic, "when the cows were too
poor to give much milk."[5]

"Common belief used to be that witches could milk a towel and get
milk from it, but people never looked for logical explanations,"[6] claimed
another old-timer who had invited us over to talk to him about bygone
days. Born in 1894, he had lived in his present house on the Upper Georges
Valley Road in Centre County since 1916 and was well versed in the legendary lore of his beloved valley.

We spent a pleasant summer afternoon on the old man's front porch
just enjoying the view of hazy mountains in the distance and listening to
his many tales, but his story of how Mary Ripka saw her neighbor milking
a towel one day proved to be one of his most fascinating accounts.

It seems that a family named Ludwig originally lived in the old man's
house, and in a homestead not far down the road to the east lived their
neighbors, Billy and Mary Ripka. It's not known any more today whether
she was naturally nosy and often spied on her neighbor or whether she

4. Stevenson W. Fletcher, *Pennsylvania Agriculture and Country Life, 1640–1840*, 506–507.
5. Ibid.
6. Charles Zettle (born May 13, 1894), interviewed April 6, 1985, and July 5, 1985.

Old-time Farm Wagon Near Frenchville. Driving through the small Clearfield County town of Frenchville one Saturday afternoon, my wife and I noticed this antique wagon sitting in a front yard. Obviously an old-time farm wagon, complete with wooden-spoked wheels, the conveyance is no doubt just like those that figure so prominently in legends about wagons whose teams of horses were sometimes rendered immobile as the result of a witch's evil spell.

just happened to wander past the Ludwig house when Mrs. Ludwig was wringing milk from a towel, but Mary Ripka would later tell her friends that one afternoon she saw Mrs. Ludwig milking a towel just like witches were supposed to do.

"This was in the days before they had cream separators," explained our storyteller. "Women would put milk in crocks and let it stand until the cream floated to the top. Then they'd take a cloth like a cheesecloth and use it to skim off the cream. Then they'd take the cloth with cream in it and wring it out into a pan or another container. I think this is what Mary Ripka saw Mrs. Ludwig doing,"[7] concluded our raconteur as he ended the little tale that was proof enough for him that people certainly did not look for logical explanations behind the old witch tales.

Ancient superstitions did seem to rule many peoples' minds at one time here in Pennsylvania, even when there were obvious logical explanations for events attributed to witchcraft. Back then if it looked like someone was using witchcraft to milk a towel, it apparently didn't occur to those

7. Ibid.

who saw the witch that the person might just be doing something quite harmless.

Using a cheesecloth as a way to separate cream from milk was a common household practice before technology found a better way to do it, and when a good Pennsylvania Dutch *hausfrau* made her *schmeerkase* she could also be seen squeezing excess milk out of the ball of cottage cheese that she had wrapped in a piece of cheese cloth to hold it together. Nonetheless, there were those who preferred to ignore these logical explanations and cling to their convictions that a witch could easily milk a towel. Although that's not a belief that lasted through the twentieth century, there was another witchcraft belief that lingers yet today, even though it's not taken as seriously anymore as it once was.

Now only regarded by most as an old superstition, the idea that bad luck will befall a person if a sable cat crosses in front of them was no doubt rooted in and fueled by the connection that many believed existed between a witch and a black cat. Witches were believed to be lovers of the night, for it was then, under the cover of darkness, that they could have their frolics and perform their evil deeds without being detected. It was because of this reputation that nocturnal animals like bats and owls were sometimes linked to them as well, but it was the black cat that was most often associated with witches.

Referred to as the witch's familiar, a sable feline's color apparently reminded people of a witch's black dress, and its ability to slink silently and effortlessly through total darkness also probably contributed to people's belief that a black cat was a witch's favorite means of carrying out some of her most dastardly deeds. As a result, many of the old witch tales center on this idea, and even carry it a step further. "When a witch disappears, a black cat appears,"[8] was once a favorite saying in the Pennsylvania hills, and there were many accounts that were touted as factual examples of these transformations.

One example of an anecdote that today would be classified as farfetched, but which many once considered as proof that witches could assume the shape of a black cat in order to torment their neighbors, was a tale that, over seventy-five years ago, was a favorite spook story that was often told around All Souls Night in the small Centre County village of

---

8. Edwin Valentine Mitchell, *It's an Old Pennsylvania Custom*, 183.

Rebersburg. There it was said that there was once a young couple, descendants of the old German stock that first settled the area, who heard their baby crying shortly after they had put it to bed.

Nothing appeared to be amiss when the husband and wife quietly peeked into the baby's room, but then, in the eerie glow of their lantern's light, they gasped in horror as they saw a black cat sitting on their baby's chest. At that moment the cat turned its head, and the distraught parents could see its eyes glowing menacingly in the soft yellow light of their lantern.

Quick as a flash and without a sound, the cat then jumped down off the baby's crib and onto the wooden floor of the cabin. Pausing just long enough to glare defiantly at the baby's parents one more time, the cat then hissed at them before shrinking in size until it was small enough to escape through a small knothole in the floor. When the parents rushed over to their baby's crib, they found that the poor child had died.

Those who believed the tale later claimed that the cat had really been a witch. She had, they claimed, first changed herself into a black cat and then entered the room by shrinking herself in size until she was small enough to squeeze up through the knothole in the floor. Once inside, she then grew back to a normal-sized cat, but after killing the child and being discovered by its parents, the witch in feline form shrunk herself until she was small enough to fit back down through the knothole.[9]

Witches did not change themselves into cats just to torment children, or so one old witch tale from Clinton County would have us believe. Down in Hopple Hollow, a quaint Clinton County section of forestland just north of the Sugar Valley Mountains and south of Bald Eagle State Forest lands, there were once many families who believed in the powers witches could exercise if they wanted to torment someone, especially neighbors with whom they had quarreled. A story of one witch's dispute with her neighbors was once a very popular account in this area, and it is still vividly remembered today by those who grew up here and heard the many witch tales that originated in the region.

Exactly how the argument started, or what it was about, has been forgotten over the years, but for whatever the reason, two families living in Hopple Hollow in the mid to late 1800s began quarreling. The Bowers'

9. Paul Rishel (born February 26, 1932), interviewed by phone August 8, 2000.

long-standing disagreement with their neighbors may have been over something major like property lines, but it could have just as easily been over a trivial matter as well.

In any case it turned out that their neighbor's wife was known as a hex who was well versed in the Black Arts. It was probably this woman's reputation, along with a feeling of guilt about having fallen out with their former good friends, that began to prey upon the Bowers' minds and caused them to imagine things, or perhaps they were never sound sleepers to start with, but shortly after the quarrel started, the Bowers claimed they could get no rest at night.

If it had happened only once they probably could have explained it away as imagination, but the tale the Bowers supposedly told was that every night when they retired for the evening, they would feel something fall down on their bed just as soon as one of them reached over and turned off the kerosene lamp on the nightstand.

As soon as they felt what they described as this "jumping down," they would immediately light the kerosene lamp to see what had happened, but to their continuing dismay they could never find a cause for the strange occurrence. When pressed for more details by those who heard the story, the Bowers would say that the disturbance felt and sounded just like it would have if a "big cat" had jumped down on their bed.[10]

Whether the cat hex forced the Bowers to settle their dispute with their neighbors may never be known, but witches who changed themselves into black cats were certainly not always successful in their reasons for doing so, or at least that's the picture that many of the other old witch tales like to paint.

In these eerie accounts, people oftentimes prepared a nasty reception for a black cat they thought was really a witch, and one such tale was once widely circulated in and around the little town of Tower City (or "Tar" City as it comes out when locals pronounce the name) in Schuylkill County.

Living in a small home on the 700 block of East Grand Avenue of Tower City in the late 1940s was an elderly lady who was feared as a witch. Her domicile was not a friendly looking house, its peeling paint and sagging, moss-covered roof giving it the appearance of a place to avoid. The old crone seemed to enjoy her privacy almost as much she seemed to relish

---

10. Margaret Ferree, recorded May 28, 2002.

A witch feeding her "familiars." Depiction from an English illustration done in the late 16th century. In this case the "familiars" are not the typical bats, owls, or black cats normally thought of as a witch's animal companions.

her reputation as a hex; a reputation that still lives on today in the minds of those who knew her when they were children, and who were told by their parents to walk to the other side of the street when they saw her coming. Today some of those same children, now grown to adulthood, no longer remember the witch's name, but they do remember that she looked the part.

"She was an old hag, really old looking; kind of hunched over and with gray, scraggly hair," was the way one man described her when he was telling me the tale of the Tower City witch. "She normally wore gray or black, and always had a staff in her hand. We were told not to look at her too," he continued. "Any kid who would see an old-fashioned card of a witch, an old Halloween card, would know exactly what this woman looked like!"[11]

Her appearance was not the main reason people didn't like her. "She was always trying to annoy her neighbors and come into their houses," claimed the man who had grown up in the house across the street from the woman. "One of the incidents I remember very well is the fact that my grandmother told my mother to put a broom across the door and she could not come in," he continued. "And this my mother would do, and the woman would go away!"[12]

The broom blockade kept the witch at bay, but did not render her powerless, or at least that's what Annie Laing thought when her daughter-in-law

---

11. William Laing (born January 15, 1942), recorded October 28, 1998.
12. Ibid.

complained that she was not sleeping well at night. Annie Laing was versed in the "white arts," and as a powwow doctor, she felt she knew who had placed a spell on her daughter-in-law, and she was equally sure how to counteract it.

"She told my mother that she should take the twenty-third Psalm in the New Testament and open it and lay it under her pillow," noted the man who had seen the strange events unfold. "She said that if she did this, she'd get all the rest that she needed and that the person that was putting the spell on her would not sleep. Well, after that, when you looked across the street, the light was on in the night, all night!"[13]

That was not the end of the Laing family's battle with the witch, however. It was as though Annie Laing's counterspell was a declaration of war, because it wasn't long after that that the Laings noticed a stranger in their yard.

"Finally, one day there was a black cat that came out of nowhere," recalled Annie Laing's grandson, still vividly remembering the incident some fifty years after he had seen it firsthand. "My grandmother said it had to be the woman across the street," he continued. "So, she said, 'When she comes, you pour boiling hot water on the cat, and it'll go away.'"[14]

It wasn't long afterwards that the mysterious black cat appeared again, causing a flurry of activity in the Laing kitchen, where they immediately put a pan of water on their stove to bring it to a boil. Once the water began to steam and bubble, the pan was removed from the red-hot stove burner and carried outside.

Carefully, and with some trepidation, Ruth Laing managed to get close enough to the unfortunate cat to throw the hot liquid onto its right side. That was all that was needed to teach the old hex across the street not to bother her neighbors again, or so it appeared to many of them, because the very next day they saw her with her right arm all bandaged up due to a burn she had somehow received the day before. The burn appeared to be right where the cat had been hit with the hot water.

When the old crone died, people were still reluctant to enter her home. The window shutters on the outside of the house had always been kept

13. Ibid.
14. Ibid.

shut, but on the day she died they were said to have mysteriously swung open. Eventually there were those brave enough to go inside the dark old manse, and when they sorted through the deceased's things, they found many items of hexerei, including the Sixth and Seventh Books of Moses.

It was the discovery of these two volumes that convinced non-believers that the old lady had indeed been a hex after all. The Books of Moses supposedly contained some of the most powerful incantations and spells used by those who practiced the Black Arts, and these volumes were placed in a pile in the back yard and burned along with the other items of hexerei found in the lady's house.

Little wonder that superstitions about witchcraft hung on as long as they did. Individuals like the Tower City witch made it difficult for people to shake off old witchcraft beliefs that had been handed down to them by their parents and grandparents. Even after the Tower City witch died in the late 1940s there were those in Tower City who were convinced that something more had to be done than just burning her books and items of hexerei. Accordingly, an exorcism was performed on her home at that time, but her power to strike fear in others has not yet been diminished, even to this day.

"Even now as we're speaking," interjected the man who knew the old witch personally, as he paused to reflect a moment before concluding his narrative, "it kinda makes the hair stand up on the back of my head a little!"[15]

15. Ibid.

CHAPTER 10

ROCKS OF AGES

Lovers of Pennsylvania place names have no doubt wondered about the origin of the name of the little town in Huntingdon County called Warriors Mark. Founded in 1768, this quaint mountain community is located to the south of the nearby Bald Eagle Mountains and just a few miles west of picturesque Half Moon Valley in Centre County.

Although the origin of the name Warriors Mark is not as certain, authorities do agree that the name of neighboring Half Moon Valley originated from the many carvings shaped like half-moons the early settlers here found on the valley's trees. Although they were able to learn that the tree decorations were made by Indians of the area, the pioneers could never determine the meaning of the symbols.

Similarly, there are those who say that trees near the town of Warriors Mark once displayed other Indian carvings whose meanings were equally mysterious. Early Huntingdon County historians like J. Simpson Africa and Albert Rung make mention of these "warriors' marks" in their histories of the area and offer them as the most likely explanation for the choice of the town's title. However, older residents of the area maintain to this day that neither Africa nor Rung got it right; that there is another explanation as to which warriors marks were really the ones from which the town took its unusual name.

Those who like to explore the back paths and little-traveled byways of the Pennsylvania countryside may already be familiar with state Route 350, which connects the villages of Spring Mount and Warriors Mark

in Huntingdon County. The pretty little country highway skirts broad
expanses of tilled fields and passes well-kept farms, taking a traveler back
to a time when developments had not yet become the dominant feature of
the countryside.

Also figuring prominently in the scenery, the dark expanse of Tussey
Mountain to the south and the well-wooded slopes of the Bald Eagle Ridge
to the north are other scenic attractions that can draw a traveler's attention
away from less noticeable points of interest along the way, like the name of
another country road that cuts off the state road and leads to points east.

Indian Tree Lane may not be noticed at all by most people who travel
through here the first time. There is a street sign with the name displayed
upon it at the mouth of the road, but lots of people probably think it's
just another common highway sign and don't even give it a second glance.
But by ignoring the byway, they are missing the opportunity to see an old
landmark that is a remarkable survivor of a much earlier day.

The first tendency many alert Route 350 travelers might have, upon
seeing the sign for Indian Tree Lane, is to head east on this road to seek
out the old tree that the road must be named after. However, the tree in
question sits back in the woods on the west side of Route 350, diagonally
northwest of the entrance to the Lane.

Even if someone knows where to look, the old oak tree is not easily
seen; unless winter is approaching and the higher bushes along the highway
have been killed off by the onslaught of the cold frosts of late fall, and the
trees here have been stripped of their colorful autumn leaves by those same
wintry frosts.

Even then, when it's no longer protected from view by the leaves on
the trees between it and the state road, the ancient oak may still be ignored
by passersby because they think it looks just like any other old tree. If they
knew the story behind the ancient forest monarch, on the other hand, they
might stop and try to see it from a closer vantage point; try to determine
for themselves if the evidence is there to support what locals say is the true
origin of the name Warriors Mark.

According to those local accounts, the Route 350 oak is the last standing
survivor of four oaks which once stood at this spot, each tree forming the
corner of a rectangular area where natives once camped. It was within this

area that the Indians often danced around their campfires and rehearsed their warrior games, one of which was target practice. And the targets, the warriors' marks at which they used to throw their tomahawks, were stones that were lodged in a hollow spot in each of the four oaks.

Three of the four oaks are gone now, but up until about forty years ago an original warriors' mark stone could still be seen, lodged in a hollow area of the remaining oak. Now the old stone relic is gone as well, to the chagrin of locals, surreptitiously carried to an Indian museum in the midwest. There the stone can be seen today, which, along with the still-living oak tree used to hold the warriors' marks, proves that the past is never really that far away.[1]

Although the Warriors Mark oak is a surprising and unusual surviving link to the natives who first greeted pioneers upon their arrival into the Pennsylvania mountain wilderness, there are other similar firsthand links that still exist as well. Some of these are even more intriguing as far as the local color and oral history that surrounds them; like the artifact discovered by road crew workers when they were building the highway that connects the villages of Wingate and Snow Shoe in the northern Allegheny Mountains of Centre County.

Present-day Route 144 is a typical Pennsylvania mountain highway, running through thick forest lands for miles and then passing by places where the trees have been cleared away to reveal inspiring panoramic overlooks of mountain ranges flowing into one another like vast ocean waves in a distant mist-covered sea. Place names along this stretch of roadway, like Gum Stump and Devil's Elbow, also tweak the imagination and cause the traveler to appreciate these mountains even more.

The hollows and ridges through here seem to have been a spot much appreciated by the Indians of the area as well, for it was along this same route that they chose a site for one of their most hallowed spots: a burial ground for their loved ones. And it was also near this same plot that they found a cave in the rocks where they could find shelter or store some of their favorite possessions; or at least that could be a conclusion that could be drawn, based on the interesting stone found in that cave by highway workers building the Wingate/Snow Shoe link of present-day Route 144 in the 1840s.

---

1. Wilson Catherman (born 1929), interviewed December 31, 1999.

Whether the natives interred their dead in the cave or not has apparently never been determined. However, an unusual artifact that was found in the cave may be suggestive. The artifact appears to be a tribute to one member of their tribe; a work of art left here by someone who apparently admired the woman to such a degree that they went to a great deal of work to create it. Painstakingly etched onto a flat piece of black rock, the woman's profile and headdress are clearly visible. If it was intended as a memorial, then this simple tribute has fulfilled its mission. Like the warriors mark rock from the old oak tree in Huntingdon County, it has survived down to the present time, thus keeping alive the memory of the natives who once walked upon the same ground over which we tread today.

Although presently in a private collection in the family of the man who found the stone in the cave, it is hoped that this unusual piece of Indian artwork will also eventually find its way into a museum where it can be more widely appreciated by future generations.

There is one other old rock with links to Pennsylvania's Indian heritage that also might be safer in a museum, but moral principles demand that, because it is a tombstone, it should remain undisturbed. It's surprising, given the many decades it's been standing there along Antes Creek, that this ancient memorial has managed to remain free of vandalism or has not been stolen by selfish individuals who either want to sell it for profit or make it a part of their own personal collections.

Without a doubt, one reason the sacred marker has been so safe is probably because it sits in such an out-of-the-way spot. However, the other reason it has survived over the years is because people have no idea that such a plain looking vertical shaft of stone marks the final resting-place of an Indian chief.

Another warrior's resting place did capture the interest of Count Louis Nicholas Zinzendorf, founder of the Moravian religious sect, when he visited the Indian village of Ostonwakin, present day Montoursville, near the mouth of Loyalsock Creek, Lycoming County, in October 1742. Here he was awakened one morning by the sounds of a woman wailing over the grave of her husband.

The incident was poignant enough that the Count noted it in the diary he kept throughout his forty years of missionary work among the Indians. It was this incident that also prompted him to record a notation concerning the burial customs of the Indians as far as their practice of erecting "either a stone or a mound in honor of their deceased heroes."[2]

Perhaps such a gravestone had been placed over the burial plot from where Zinzendorf heard the wails of the grieving widow that early October morning, but no doubt that gravesite and its stone marker have since been forgotten and covered over by the works of man or by the inexorable forces of nature. However, one striking example of the type of Indian tombstone referred to by Zinzendorf can still be found near the impressive Sanderson mansion in Nippenose Valley of Lycoming County.

Built by financier George L. Sanderson in 1874, the house sits on the impressive Lochabar estate located midway between the villages of Rauchtown and Antes Fort. Here, along the banks of Antes Creek and near the unfailing, ever-flowing Indian spring, the largest in Pennsylvania, is the gravesite of Wi-daagh, a sachem of the Conestoga Indians who died with a heavy heart.

The deep green waters of Chief Wi-daagh's spring add a nice touch of color to the surrounding mountains, especially in the fall when the artists of autumn paint the leaves with brilliant splashes of gold, red, and orange. But Wi-daagh's spirit probably doesn't notice the uplifting colors, nor would it be calmed by the soft murmurs of the creek that flows by its resting place.

At least, that could be the conclusion that some might reach when they learn that, on September 13, 1700, it was Wi-daagh that traded away all the Susquehanna River lands through here to William Penn "in consideration of a parcel of English goods."[3]

It was no doubt one of the most lop-sided deals in the history of real estate transactions. For in exchange for what was probably nothing more than a few trinkets, beads, and bolts of brightly colored cloth, Wi-daagh managed to hand over to Penn a territory that had been in Indian hands for centuries, and which they would never be able to call their own again. But despite Wi-daagh's mismanagement of Indian interests, time and his fellow tribesmen seem to have forgiven him his errors.

When the old chief died, he was buried near where he lived, by the spring that bears his name today. And as evidence of the respect with which

---

2. John F. Meginness, *Otzinachson*, 104.
3. Ibid, 21.

they regarded him, Wi-daagh's tribe erected a large vertical shaft of stone over his grave, and it is that shaft of stone that still attracts Native American visitors today.

They come to offer their respects, smoke the pipe of peace, and, in Indian fashion, pay tribute to the north, south, east and west. Sometimes the evidence of those ceremonies can be seen when a visit is paid to Wi-daagh's grave; reminders just like the one visitors to the gravesite would have found, if they had stopped there in the spring of 2000.

Lying at the foot of the tombstone at that time were the remains of a peace pipe, placed there by one of the Indians who still feels a need to honor the memory of this maligned chieftain. It is perhaps those ceremonies and those respectful visits that have enabled the old sachem's spirit to find eternal rest at last.

There is yet another rock of ages that has a connection with the Indian days here in Pennsylvania; and it also is a gravestone, but that of an early settler who too was wronged. Almost as well off the beaten path as Wi-daagh's grave, the grave of Christophel Hennig is one of many other forgotten burial plots that form one of the oldest burial grounds in Centre County.

Like the ancient "windy city" of Troy, made famous by the Greek poet Homer in his *Iliad*, the old cemetery is situated on a high bluff on a farm in Haines Township of Centre County; and here, just like at Troy, no matter in which direction you look there are beautiful views of the surrounding countryside. But there are other similarities between this place of the dead and the celebrated Greek city of Troy, including the winds that never seem to rest, and a heroine to take the place of the beautiful Helen of Troy, heroine of the Trojan Wars.

Preserved on the back of Christophel Hennig's will is the record of an incident that will not be found in any of the histories of Pennsylvania's wars with the Indians, including Loudon's *Narratives* or Sipe's *Indian Wars*. It is just one more example of how accounts of many of these episodes from the days of Pennsylvania's border wars never made it into the history books and have only survived through the oral traditions of individual families. It also preserves the memory of the old Revolutionary War veteran's daughter, who, just like Helen of Troy, was taken prisoner in a time of war.

According to the notes on the back of Christophel's will, while the rest of his family was cutting grain one day during harvest time in the 1770s, his daughter Margaret was at home preparing the evening meal. When the family quit for the day and came back from the fields to eat supper, a scene of devastation greeted them.

Where their cabin once stood, they found a burnt shell; and even more heart-rending was the realization that there was no trace of the young woman who had been left there alone. There was nothing the family could do just then but mourn the loss of their unfortunate daughter, pray for her safe return, and start rebuilding their cabin. Pray and rebuild they did, and hardy pioneers that they were, they lost no time to begin to search for their loved one.

There was no doubt that the defenseless woman had been kidnapped by Indians who were fighting on the British side of the Revolutionary War, but it took the Hennigs two years to learn that she had been taken to an Indian village somewhere in New York State. Soon after this glimmer of hope was raised, two of Christophel's sons, who both had served in the same Revolutionary War company as their father, immediately set out to bring back their sister. It was to be a long and dangerous undertaking.

When they finally located the Indian village, the Hennig brothers found not one, but two white women there who had been captured by tribal raiding parties. Although the men didn't recognize her at first glance, they finally realized that one of the captives was their sister Margaret.

In the two years she had been with her Indian captors, she had married an Indian chief and had born him two children. For all appearances she was now an Indian herself, dressing like them and having fully learned their language and their customs. But it wasn't enough to sway her kinfolk. Being fearless frontiersmen, Margaret's brothers dismissed the close bonds that now tied her to the Indians and told her captors that they had come to take her home.

It was not a declaration that was appreciated by the Indians, who, after a brief council, replied in no uncertain terms that "if the men left with her, they would follow, and nobody would get home." The Hennigs, apparently blessed with some natural hostage negotiation skills, finally, after some further discussion, got the Indians to agree that Margaret and her brothers could return home, accompanied by her husband. And so it was that the young mountain maid was brought back home to the joyful cries and open arms of her parents and siblings.

There are no further details, either recorded on Christophel's will or supplied through oral history, that describe what the Hennig family's reaction was, when they discovered that their daughter had borne children to the Indian who came back with her the day she stepped out of what had seemed to be the jaws of death.

The family accounts do say that Margaret was buried in the same cemetery where Christophel rests today, while her Indian husband rests just outside the perimeter, in non-hallowed ground. There is no way to tell for sure, since sometime in the 1920s a previous owner of the farm removed two and a half rows of tombstones, including Margaret's and her husband's, presumably to obtain a few more square feet of land on which to grow crops.

The Hennig-Neidig cemetery, as it's now known, was neglected for many decades, until recent efforts by local resident Randall Stover restored it to presentable shape once more. The old gentleman has become the unofficial caretaker of the burying ground and has declared that he will

View of the Hennig-Neidig Cemetery. Last resting place of some of the first settlers in Penns Valley, Centre County, and of the Indian who figured so prominently in their family history.

Gravestones in the Hennig-Neidig Cemetery. The old graveyard is the resting place not only of Christophel Hennig but of numerous veterans of the Revolutionary War as well. It also could be that the two sunken headstones alone in the corner are those of Christophel's daughter Margaret and her Indian husband, lying side-by-side for eternity.

someday replace the tombstones that were so callously removed by the former owner of the farm. It is a commendable and worthwhile undertaking, and one we hope he can accomplish in the time he has left.

Although the tombstones he places there will not be as old as the other rocks of ages that have been discussed in this essay, they will nonetheless preserve the memories of those, native Americans and colonists alike, whose lives and times deserve to be remembered for their place in a significant part of Pennsylvania's thrilling colonial past.

NOTE: Randall Stover has kept a diary of his efforts to restore the Hennig-Neidig cemetery and has also compiled a history of the place. When handing out copies of his compilation he also includes a sliver from a limb off an old red oak tree that was just a young sapling when Christophel Hennig was buried next to it in 1790.

As the small tree grew into the mighty oak it is today, there grew along with it, along the entire center of one of its limbs, an image of a star with beams of light extending out from it. It is a unique work of natural art, and is perhaps meant as a sign that as long as there is love, there is a glimmer of hope for all mankind, despite our seemingly inescapable inability to live in peace.[4]

Chief Wi-daagh's Grave. As it still stands along Antes Creek in Lycoming County, this monolith preserves the memory of an Indian chief whose skill in negotiating real estate deals left much to be desired.

4. Randall Stover (born October 20, 1919), recorded September 25, 1999.

Chief Wi-daagh's Grave Closeup. A closer view of this remarkable landmark. The day I took this picture there was still evidence of a tobacco offering burnt there by some of the old chiefs admirers and possibly a few of his fellow Native Americans.

The Indian Oak. It was this tree and its three fallen companions, and their stone targets, that some believe are the basis for the name of the nearby town of Warriors Mark in Huntingdon County.

The Indian Oak – a closeup view. The dark elliptical spot above the large hollow in the tree was where local Indian warriors used to place flat stones which they used as targets, or "marks," when practicing their tomahawk throwing skills in preparation for war.

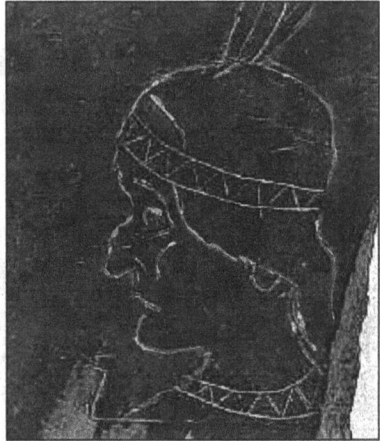

Face of the Indian Maiden. Sometime in the 1840's, highway workers found this engraved stone in a cave along present-day Route 144 in the Allegheny Mountains north of Milesburg in Centre County. Who she was, and why someone regarded her so highly as to take the time to etch her likeness in this stone will probably never be known. Note the size of the stone relative to the three fingers supporting it at the top so a photo could be taken.

Face of the Indian Maiden – closer view. She was not a beauty by today's standards, but she was respected highly enough that someone felt her memory should be preserved in this "rock of ages."

CHAPTER 11

STRETCHING IT

Loose ends, unsolved puzzles, and unresolved issues of any kind are an annoyance to many people, and most folks like to tie up loose ends rather than letting them hang. Likewise, it seems that human nature drives most of us to find solutions to puzzles instead of letting them get the best of us; to affect some sort of closure to open-ended situations in preference to walking away from them. It's these same kinds of personal characteristics, the stubborn determination and the love of solving mysteries and problems that led me, I guess, to examine my collection of Pennsylvania legends and folktales the way I have.

Readers of my previous volumes already are aware that I treat each tale I collect as a little mystery, trying to discover if the story has any basis in fact; attempting to find the kernels of truth that may be buried within the account, no matter how tall it may seem. Some of the old tales seem to stretch the truth to the limit; are so outrageous that they are obviously exaggerations intended only to amuse and entertain. It is these types of tales that tend to cast doubts on the believability of other folktales, legends, and pieces of oral history that may, in fact, have some truth upon which they're based.

Even documented historical accounts seem like exaggerations at times when they're compared to actual tall tales. In Miss Blackman's *History of Susquehanna County*, for example, there are accounts describing the prevalence of rattlesnakes noticed by pioneer settlers in that county around 1780, when rattlers sung in farmers' barns and "made music" in their hay fields. Here, near present-day Red Rock, Luzerne County, one hot August afternoon, a group of huckleberry pickers, after filling their pails, "went to killing rattlesnakes." According to one first-hand account, the snake hunters killed, in the span of a few hours, a total of 444 rattlers, 411 of which were young ones.[1]

Philip Tome, the great pioneer hunter of Lycoming County and author of *Pioneer Life*, that colorful record of early hunting days in this part of Pennsylvania during the 1790s and early 1800s, mentions similar instances of large masses of rattlesnakes he and others saw sunning themselves on rocks along Pine Creek near his homestead at present-day Waterville. Tome claims to have seen forty on one rock at a time and says he "heard others tell of seeing three hundred together."[2] However, on the very next page of his account he also mentions having seen hoop snakes, which he also refers to as "horn" snakes; that reptile that often was the subject of snake tales of the tallest variety.

The old hunter describes the hoop snake in great detail, noting that they were "very rare," about five feet long, and similar in color to a yellow rattlesnake. He also claims they had a tail terminating "in a black horn, four or five inches in length, and very sharp at the point," with venom so deadly that "it is even fatal to trees." Tome goes on to note that he saw first-hand an instance when one such snake bent itself into a circular form and rolled over the ground like a hoop in order to attack a man.

The man, says Tome, managed to step aside and avoid the snake, but the snake was rolling at such a rate of speed it could not stop, and "struck its horn into an elm tree with such force that it could not extricate it." "The snake," claims Tome, "died, hanging there, in two weeks, and the tree was lifeless at the end of a month."[3]

Tales of hoop snakes and other exaggerated accounts like this tended to be a common topic of conversation in lumber camps, hunters' shanties, barrooms, and with loafers relaxing around the potbelly stoves of country stores. It was when you got into these arenas that tales tended to get stretched to the limit, and perhaps Phillip Tome included one such tale in his book just to poke fun at his readers.

---

1. Emily C. Blackman, *History of Susquehanna County, Pennsylvania*, 57.
2. Philip Tome, *Pioneer Life or Thirty Years a Hunter*, 114–116.
3. Ibid.

*The Old Potbelly Stove.
It sat for years in Jodon's General
Store in Spring Mills, Centre County.
When I took this photo the old relic
and its surroundings looked pretty
much the same way they did when
"Pud" Myers owned the store half
a century earlier and old-timers
gathered around the stove on cold
winter days to spin their tales.*

*The Old Potbelly Stove.
Artist's rendition of the same.
(Drawn by James J. Frazier.)*

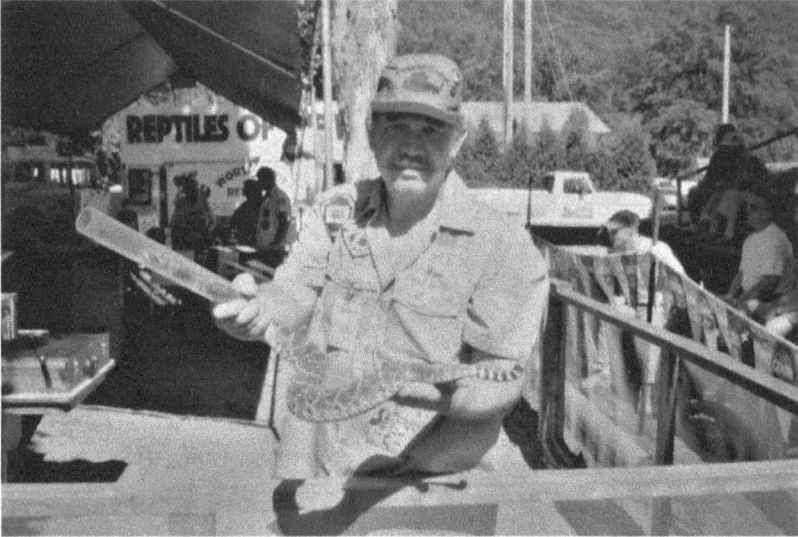

One Big Snake. Larger-than-life reptiles like this monster are shown at Cross Fork in Potter County during the annual rattlesnake hunt held there every June. Perhaps it was a snake of this size that once gave someone the idea for one of the tall tales about the size of Pennsylvania's rattlesnakes or for another snake story that stretched the truth so it would be more entertaining to those who heard it.

Another One. A snake handler at Cross Fork showing a large rattlesnake captured during the annual snake hunt at this quaint mountain retreat.

If so, he would have been welcomed with open arms into the Tall Tale Club of the seventeenth century, members of which enjoyed entertaining one another with stories that stretched both the truth and their imaginations. Among their stretches were exaggerated descriptions of the rattlesnakes of provincial Pennsylvania.

"There is here," claimed John Campanius, when describing his travels through the province during the years 1642 to 1648, "a large and horrible serpent which is called a rattlesnake." "It has a head like that of a dog and can bite off a man's leg as clear as if it had been hewn down with an axe," claimed the European traveler, who ended his description of the terrifying serpents by noting that they grew to a length of three yards and were "as thick as the thickest part of a man's leg!"[4]

Those who were familiar with rattlesnakes and their prevalence during pioneer days were no doubt amused by Campanius' descriptions, realizing in the end that he was just another good raconteur; a storyteller who espoused English lexicographer Samuel Johnson's philosophy that "seldom is any good story wholly true." It was a philosophy that was embraced by the best storytellers, and it resulted in many colorful accounts. I've been told a number of these Pennsylvania tall tales during my thirty years of canvassing the state for material for my books, and what follows are some of those exaggerated stories.

THE STRETCHING BOARD
(Warriors Mark, Huntingdon County)

"Fella up here had this old coon dog, and he said he was really good. He said all he had to do was put out a stretcher the size of the coon he wanted for him to get, and he said he'd go, and it'd take him maybe a couple days, but he said he'd always come back with a coon that would fit that stretcher. But he said one night his wife went and left the darn ironing board out on the back porch. And he said, 'I told her, don't ever let that ironing board out!' And he said that dog went out, and he said 'you know he was gone for two years; he went way above Tipton somewhere.' And he said he got this coon, and he brought him back, and the coon fit the board! But he said that dog wasn't so dumb. He drug the coon half ways on the one way

---

4. Stevenson W. Fletcher, *Pennsylvania Agriculture and Country Life, 1640–1840*, 73.

and turned him around and drug him the other way, and so didn't wear out the fur!"[5]

GRINDING TO A HALT
(Buffalo Run Valley, Centre County)

"Guy come in here one day, he had a little farm, and he said 'boy I went home after work last night, and I wanted to grind some chop'. He said, 'I got an old model T Ford; I took the back wheel off and have it hooked up with a pulley to my grinder.' And he said, 'Did you ever work around those model Ts?'

And I said, 'No, I never played with 'em.' 'Well,' he said, 'the dang things have a habit of runnin' backwards every once in a while. They'll backfire and run backwards.' He said, 'you know that thing backfired and got to runnin' backward, and I just un-ground nineteen bushels of corn!'"[6]

A MIGHTY BIG DEER
(Gatesburg, Centre County)

"Neighbor back here said that when he first got the piece of ground there was a report of a big buck back there, and he said he made up his mind he wanted to shoot it. He seen it the first year and didn't get a shot at it, but the second year he was after it, he got it. He said it was too big to drag out of the woods. It was a big buck! So he said he took his camera back and took a picture of it, and he said the picture weighed five pounds!"[7]

A LONG STRETCH TO HOME
(Haines Township, Centre County)

During the days when it was considered a sport to see who could tell the biggest lie, a man near Aaronsburg let this one fly, one afternoon. The old storyteller told of the day he had taken a team of horses and wagon to Bellefonte for a load of logs and got caught in a severe downpour on the way back. Not only had he gotten drenched, he recalled, but the horse harness stretched so much that the team got home "a day and a half ahead

5. Allen Harpster (born March 21, 1932), recorded December 28, 1999.
6. Ibid.
7. Ernest Harpster (born January 6, 1938), recorded December 28, 1999.

of the wagon!" It is not recorded whether the man who told this story was given the title of the biggest liar for that day or not.[8]

AN ETERNAL FLAME
(Waynesboro, Franklin County)

"This Merv Kauffmann, he used to tell some of the biggest lies you ever wanted to hear in your life! He told me one time he was up there to the Waynesboro impounding dam on South Mountain, where Waynesboro gets their water supply from. He said he was up there fishin' and it was nighttime, and he said he had a lantern with him and the fishin' rod stickin' through the lantern. He went back into the woods to take a leak, and here a fish jumped on the pole, and pulled both the pole and the lantern into the water. He lost his fishin' pole and he lost his lantern both. He said two weeks later he went down fishin', and he caught a fish, and while he was pullin' this fish in, he pulled his other fishin' line in and the lantern. And he said the lantern was still lit!"[9]

QUITE A MOUTHFUL
(Somewhere on Penn's Creek, Centre County)

"I have one more, about a boy fishing on Penn's Creek," said the local historian. He had known some of the original raftsmen who once guided log rafts down the Susquehanna during the nineteenth century lumber boom here in Pennsylvania, and he had listened to and preserved many of their stories of the old rafting days. But this tale of the young fisherman was one he had heard from a coworker not too many years ago.

"The boy dug up some bait and put what he thought were worms in a can," continued the river man. "In fact when I was a kid, when I went fishin', I'd carry the worms in a can with some moss in it. And this boy would put these freshly dug worms on the hook, and every time he did, the worms would bite him. Here, I guess, the way the story goes, he used up all his worms, and there was quite a number of them. He started to get sick, and the very next day he died. Here what he was using was baby copperheads!"

8. Barbara M. Anderson, editor, *Haines Township Life and Tradition*, 76.
9. Larry Kalamer (born May 31, 1938), recorded January 25, 1998.

This little episode was related to my informant "as though it were "the Gospel truth," he recalled, and so it first sounded to him like it must have been an actual event. But when he asked a Pennsylvania Fish Commission official about the tale the commissioner just chuckled, explaining that it was nothing but a legend, "told about every stream in Pennsylvania!"[10]

MOSQUITOES TO AVOID
(Scotia Barrens, Centre County)

"There's been fishin' back there in those ponds ever since I can remember. My uncle Clair Burns owned some of that, and he used to tell a story about the mosquitoes. It's really bad back there for mosquitoes; you can imagine in the summer! He said the biggest mosquitoes he ever ran into got so bad he took a butcher kettle along with him one time and set it over top of him so he could fish and keep them away from him. But the darn mosquitoes took the butcher kettle! Anybody that goes back there and sits around in the summer, you could almost believe that!"[11]

NOT A GOOD CHEW
(Somewhere on Thickhead and Tussey Mountains, Centre County)

Although this story is not really a tall tale like the preceding ones, it does preserve an account of how one inventive lumberman stretched the truth a bit to save himself some money. The tale was related to me by a man who recalled hearing the old lumberman himself tell the story, one day in Rishel's country store near Tusseyville in Centre County.

"Old Datz Miller used to work in the lumber camps back in the Tussey Mountains, probably on Thickhead or in Treaster Kettle. He'd stay there during the week and come home on weekends. Datz liked to chew tobacco, but he'd often run out by the end of the week. When he did, he'd pluck a long hair from the tail of one of the lumber camp's horses and roll it up and put it in his mouth.

"He'd then go to another tobacco chewer and tell him he'd run out and wonder if he'd loan him a plug until the following week. The fella would give Datz a plug, and Datz would pretend to put it in his mouth.

---

10. Lynn Frank (born October 14, 1924), recorded by phone January 24, 1999.
11. Ernest Harpster (born January 6, 1938), recorded December 28, 1999.

"Datz would chew a little, and then would reach in and find the end of the horsehair ball and slowly pull the strand of hair out of this mouth. The guy he'd borrowed the plug of tobacco from would see the hair and say 'This tobacco's no good! I don't want any of this!' and throw away his pouch. Datz would look where the pouch landed and then he'd come back later, and he'd have lots of chews to last out the week!"[12]

If Datz Miller ever got caught at his little deception he never mentioned it to anyone, nor did he recall how many times he got away with it; but if he had been caught, he might have ended up in a fist fight with the chewer he tried to deceive. Daily living in the mountains in those days was not for the mellow or faint-hearted, and life in the lumber camps was no different.

The feisty lumberman apparently liked to engage in a fight at the drop of a hat, and even considered a fight or two as just another form of entertainment. In that regard, he was much like the patrons who frequented a saloon in the small village of Coburn, Centre County, around 1900. To these regulars, it was considered a "dull and disappointing night" if there was no fight![13]

A HEALTHY PLACE TO LIVE?
(Penn's Valley, Centre County)

"One time a local preacher was accompanying a newcomer into Rebersburg. They were crossing Nittany Mountain to come down into the valley, and when the man looked at the scene below, he commented that this place was so beautiful that people here must live a long time. 'Yep,' the minister replied. 'As a matter of fact, we had to shoot a few folks to start a cemetery!'"[14]

The minister's sense of humor concerning graveyards was not something new. As far back as colonial times there were people who viewed cemeteries in a lighter vein, too. Some entrepreneurs in those days, for example, seemed to think burial ground fences provided an ideal spot for some humorous advertisements, like the man who painted the following statement on a colonial graveyard fence in Chester County: "Use Jones's bottled ale if you would keep out of here!"[15]

---

12. Paul A. Rishel (born February 26, 1932), recorded by phone July 31, 2000.

13. Harry R. Burd, "Two Mountain Schools," *Centre County Heritage*, Fall 1981, 17.

14. Clarence Musser (born May 12, 1884), interviewed August 28, 1971 and November 12, 1971.

15. Grant N. Sassaman, editor, *Pennsylvania, A Guide to the Keystone State*, 413.

Advertisers were a little more sensitive in later times; a little more discreet about where they placed their signs. But even 150 years later some ad men didn't care how close their placards were to burial grounds, like the man hanging advertising posters, who wanted to place his advertisements around the graveyard at the Holy Cross Cemetery on the Upper Georges Valley Road near Spring Mills, back in the earlier decades of the last century. He was considerate enough to request permission, but he was probably taken aback at the reply he got, at least according to the following version of the tale.

"Cal Kennely was working right there in the graveyard one day. He was a caretaker, and some guy came along who was advertising the circus in Bellefonte. He wanted to put up posters to advertise the circus, and he asked Cal about putting some up around the graveyard, you know. Cal said to him, 'It won't do you any good. These people can't go!'"[16]

THE BIGGEST LIAR
(Centre, Lancaster, Lehigh, and Northampton Counties)

The story of the biggest liar could no doubt once be found in almost any county in Pennsylvania. For some reason it was quite a popular tale; most probably because those who heard it and passed it on, thought it reminded them of someone. Its universal acceptance can be easily understood when it is realized that in every community prior to the middle of the last century, there was at least one man whose reputation as the town liar outshined that of all others. And this was not a moniker to be ashamed of in those days; in fact, it was more of an accolade awarded to someone by his peers.

There was nothing peculiar about such a man. He was similar to other older men of his generation, many of whom spent some of their free time loafing around the nearest general store. Nearly every evening these local authorities on almost any subject could be found crowded around the store's customary pot-bellied stove, which usually served as the focal point for their meetings.

R. B. Mench and "Cracker" Billy Stover are remembered as storekeepers in Aaronsburg, Centre County, while Frank Carson kept store in Potters Mills. "Pud" Meyer's general store in Spring Mills was a popular gathering place as well, and today the store is still open for business, with its old

---

16. Robert F. Frazier (born July 9, 1920), recorded December 13, 1988.

pot-bellied stove in the back looking much like it did years ago, when it was a weekly Mecca for any good storyteller who lived within ten miles of the little country town.

Gatherings at these local emporiums served as a fine form of entertainment for the locals, and it is no wonder that storytelling was usually on the agenda. The better the story, the better the entertainment, and so there were no rules on how truthful a story had to be; or as one man who experienced some of those sessions firsthand described it, "All those old fellas lied!"[17]

Everyone, including the storekeepers themselves, knew that you had to be careful about what to believe and what not to believe when someone told a story around a pot-bellied stove. That's supported by the story about an amused storekeeper who once asked his crowd of loafers, "Who's going to tell the biggest one tonight?"[18] The store owner might have been none other than Coburn's Bill Crater since it was his establishment, locals say, which was a favorite hangout for the biggest liar of them all.

Among the best-known old-timers of the eastern Penn's Valley towns of Aaronsburg and Coburn, Centre County, were "Dutch John," a hobo blacksmith who frequented the area, and Mann Eisenhuth who lived way up in the mountains above Coburn. Not much is remembered anymore about Eisenhuth other than the fact that he "lied devilishly," lived near Rupp Hollow in High Valley, and oftentimes came to Bill Crater's store to loaf.

Anyone likes to see a master at work, and Bill Crater was no different, at least according to a once-popular account that made its rounds during the early 1900s. Crater apparently enjoyed hearing Mann Eisenhuth's stories, and one slow afternoon he asked him to "tell a good lie." Eisenhuth uncharacteristically brushed aside the request, saying he wasn't in the mood, since his friend Al Fowler, owner of a small sawmill in the tiny neighboring village of Ingleby, had died that morning. The news cast a decided pall over the small group of loafers in the store, and they all slowly departed in a somber mood.

Everyone remained convinced that the news of Fowler's death was absolutely true, until the "deceased" came into town that night. One local

17. Albert Mingle (born March 28, 1897), interviewed July 4, 1973.
18. Ibid.

who had heard Eisenhuth's story that afternoon was at first so taken aback when he met Fowler on the street that he was speechless. Then when he finally realized what Mann Eisenhuth had done, he could only splutter, "Why Al, I thought you died this morning!"[19]

The story of the biggest liar was once considered highly amusing and was widely circulated throughout the state, taking on the names of well-known local individuals wherever it landed. One version of the tale was once popular in Hinkletown, in Lancaster County, where it was said the biggest liar was asked, as he walked by an acquaintance who was sitting on his front porch, to "Tell me another lie."

"I don't have time now," replied the prevaricator. "Johnny W. died this morning, and I want to go down right away." Anxious to lend his sympathy and support to the deceased's family, the man on the front porch went down too, only to discover his request for another lie had been granted after all.[20]

Thomas Brendle and William Troxell, those early collectors of folk stories in the Pennsylvania Dutch regions of eastern Pennsylvania during the earlier decades of the twentieth century, included a version of the biggest liar tale in their highly enjoyable compilation published by the Pennsylvania German Society in 1944. The men collected several versions of the story, and found it to be "widely heard," "always localized," and with the name of the liar "always given."[21]

One of their versions, collected in the "western part of Lehigh County," has the biggest liar passing by the local mill and telling the miller that "John Krumm died last night." Not satisfied to let it go at that, this liar also gets the miller to volunteer to dig Krumm's grave that evening. Then several hours later John Krumm walks into the mill and the astonished miller gasps, "Why John—John—John, you are dead!"[22]

Brendle and Troxell collected another popular version of the motif in Northampton County. Here, in the town of Danielsville, the local undertaker enters a bar, sees N. N., the biggest liar, and asks him to "tell me a big

19. Ibid.
20. Larry Alexander, "Lake Woebegone Comes to Hinkletown," *Intelligencer Journal*, Lancaster County, August 14, 1997.
21. Thomas R. Brendle and William S. Troxell, "Pennsylvania German Folk Tales, Legends, Once-upon-a-time Stories, Maxims and Sayings," *Proceedings of the Pennsylvania German Society–Volume L.*, 192.
22. Ibid.

lie." Feigning relief at finally finding the undertaker, N. N. tells him that "S. G. of Wind Gap has died and you are to come and lay out the body!"

The dutiful mortician loads up his equipment and drives out to Wind Gap, only to find S. G. feeding his cattle. "Why—why—why, N. N. told me you were dead," mutters the undertaker as he finally manages to speak.

Perhaps more familiar than the undertaker with the types of storytelling that could be heard in country stores and saloons, S. G. laughingly replies "Do you believe one word of what N. N. says?"[23] It was a question that was a valid one, but one which fortunately was not often asked in those times when good stories were regularly stretched a bit. Everyone knew that the answer to the question would take all the fun out of the whole pastime.

---

23. Ibid.

CHAPTER 12

DEVIL'S FIRE (AND OTHER SUPERNATURAL PYROTECHNICS)

F ire was once regarded with superstitious awe by ancient humans, as they looked upon its dancing and flashing flames with a sense of wonder; and judging from the folktales once prevalent here in Pennsylvania, some of that deep-seated superstition survived up until relatively recent times in some of the more isolated mountainous sections of the state.

This was particularly true in the Pennsylvania Dutch regions and settlements where people clung to the old beliefs and superstitions as though they were necessary guides for avoiding harm, living successful lives, and even for becoming rich. And as far as the beliefs about becoming wealthy, there was once a notion that fire was a possible road to riches for anyone who knew its secrets.

Such tales could once be readily heard where the Blue Mountains run through the Pennsylvania Dutch lands of Berks and Lehigh Counties; and even today, if the right person is consulted, the interested listener might yet hear a tale of how someone found the Dutchman's pot of gold, that treasure trove popularly referred to in the Dutch country as *Deiwelsfeier*, or, in the English language, Devil's Fire.

Although known for the torments he enjoyed inflicting upon mankind, old Lucifer apparently was apt to bestow a reward occasionally upon those who found the fires he had built to warm himself while visiting the earthly world. At least that's the impression anyone would get, when they hear the tales of the Blue Mountains that tell of how a man was following a path through a field late one night and came upon a fire.

Although it was yet relatively small in size, it looked as if it could rapidly spread throughout the field if something wasn't done immediately. In order to extinguish the blaze, the man threw his jacket on it, thereby smothering the flames, but when he picked up his coat, he was surprised to find it "covered with pieces of gold." Others, when they heard about his experience, generally agreed that the man had been lucky enough to stumble upon a Devil's fire.[1]

In yet another tale from that same area, it is related that a belated hunter one night discovered a heap of glowing coals up on the highest ridges of the Blue Mountains. The smoldering pile of embers seemed out of place in such a remote mountainous defile, particularly at that late hour, and that fact alone would have been enough to send chills up the bravest man's spine. Whether the unusual circumstances unnerved the hunter or not is not related in the old tale, but it is stated that the dying fire was located on the spot where the last Indian of the Blue Mountains had lived, before he was set upon and torn apart by wild animals.

It would have been a hellish way to die, and that's perhaps why this story concludes by noting that when the hunter came back to this same spot the next day, he found a pile of gold instead of ashes and charred wood where he had seen the fire the night before. The blaze had been, the idea seems to be, a Devil's fire, lit by Satan himself to keep warm while he enjoyed the memories of this place; the site where his evil influences had led to the terrible suffering and death of the old Indian.[2]

Although it's hard to believe today that people could once have had these kinds of naive notions, it's probably easier to understand where such beliefs came from when fire is viewed through the eyes of those who look upon it for the first time. One such case on record is that of the Ladrones Islanders of the North Pacific.

Here, in 1521, Spanish explorer Ferdinand Magellan came ashore to rest and to stock up on food supplies before he could continue his quest to

---

1. Thomas R. Brendle and William S. Troxell, "Pennsylvania German Folk Tales, Legends, Once-upon-a-time Stories, Maxims and Sayings," *Proceedings of the Pennsylvania German Society—Volume L*, 200.

2. Ibid.

circumnavigate the globe. Plagued by the islanders' repeated thefts of his supplies, Magellan ordered one of their villages burned one day.

The idyllic conditions under which they lived had never forced the islanders to evolve much beyond the simple lifestyle they had always enjoyed; never had led them to the discovery of fire. They could only stand and marvel when they saw their wooden homes consumed by flames, and their first thought was that the fire was "a beast, which fed upon wood." Some natives, braver than the others, came close enough to the flames that they were burned, and when the others saw this, they kept their distance, fearing that if they got too close they, too, would be "devoured or poisoned by this powerful animal."[3]

No doubt these types of fears were prevalent in many ancients who tried to understand the nature and origins of fire, and it is those fears that caused people to attribute its unique properties to supernatural forces. These are the foundations, I believe, that led to stories of Devil's fire, and to other supernatural tales about fire that have arisen over the centuries, particularly those about phantom flames that are as unpredictable and unexplainable as ghosts.

Tales of ghost fires seem to be included in the legendary lore of many nations, including Scotland, where one weird legend like this was associated with Roslin Chapel in the village of Roslin, seven miles south of Edinburgh. Here it was said that the ancient cathedral, built in 1446, appeared to be engulfed in flames whenever a descendant of its founder, William St. Clair, Prince of Orkney and Duke of Oldenburgh, was about to die. It is unlikely that this quaint tale still persists today, given the fact that the last known descendant of the founder died in 1778. However, even one hundred and twenty years afterwards, sightings of the flames were still being reported and the old tradition had not yet been extinguished.[4]

The same can be said for traditions like this in Pennsylvania, where accounts of ghostly fires were still circulating up until almost the middle of the twentieth century. That they created a lasting impression on those that heard the tales is evidenced by the fact that just ten years ago I could still find people who remembered their grandparents telling the stories to them, just like the gentleman whose grandfather claimed to have seen a ghost fire himself.

---

3. Charles Hardwick, *Traditions, Superstitions, and Folk-lore*, 36–37.
4. John H. Ingram, *Haunted Homes and Family Traditions of Great Britain*, 541.

Ghost Fire. Artist's rendering of an apparition of the burning mill that some once believed could be seen near the village of Roadside in Franklin County. (Drawn by James J. Frazier)

"They used to set and tell these stories when I was a kid, and I remember them!" chuckled the Franklin County native whose grandfather once told him about a strange occurrence he had one night around 1936 along Little Antietam Creek near the village of Glen Forney.

Business had taken the gentleman into Waynesboro that day, and it was dark when he started walking toward home that same evening. It was about a six-mile hike to get back to his cozy homestead, and in the dark, it must have seemed to the tired man like it was going to be a long and boring trek. The hike started out that way, but shortly after the nocturnal sojourner passed the place where the old White Mill had once stood, near the present-day village of Roadside, he suddenly noticed a bright glow illuminating the trees ahead.

Realizing that the light was coming from behind him, the puzzled traveler turned around and saw an image of the old mill engulfed in flames. The bright yellow flames danced and flickered, casting long shadows on the roadside, just as they must have done when the mill had burnt down one night several years earlier. At first, he was surprised, but then a rush of adrenaline sent bolts of fear through the lone wayfarer, and he took off running.

At first, he was making good time going up Green Ridge, but he hadn't run far until he had to stop, because his way was blocked by a number of good-sized trees that had mysteriously fallen onto the road. It was at a spot in the road where he couldn't detour around the fallen giants without backtracking, and since that was not an inviting prospect, the frightened runner jumped across the trees, one at a time, until he was able to resume a full sprint and run back home to safety.[5]

"I don't know if he was hallucinating or what, but I never knew him to drink!" laughed my storyteller, somewhat skeptical of what he had been told. It was skepticism born of our fast-paced, money-hungry, futuristic age, and perhaps it was this modern-day unwillingness to believe in such things that finally extinguished the flames of the old White Mill's ghost fire.

It might be argued that otherworldly phenomena like this depend on worldly beliefs to sustain them, and once subjected to the cold, hard, scrutiny of dispassionate inquiry cannot very long survive. That, perhaps, is why the present generation no longer talks about or sees other ghost fires as well, like the one that some once claimed flared up occasionally just outside the small village of Woodward in Haines Township of Centre County.

It was March 5, 1896, when Haines Township's newly elected constable, John Barner, knocked on the door of local mechanic Bill Ettlinger to arrest him for jumping bail on an assault charge the previous summer. Ettlinger was known for his hot temper, and for six months he'd been terrorizing the town of Woodward.

He was a wild looking sort, with jet-black hair and a thick black mustache "that turned up at the ends."[6] Often seen skulking around town with a rifle in his hands, a pistol in his belt, and a knife hanging on his side, Ettlinger had threatened to kill anyone who tried to take him in. John Barner wasn't buying it.

Ettlinger was rarely at home anymore, spending a lot of his time in remote hideouts with caches of weapons he'd set up in the nearby mountains. The fugitive mountain man would come down out of the hills

---

5. Larry Kalamer (born May 31, 1938), recorded January 25, 1998.

6. Barbara Brueggebors, two articles: "Terror in Woodward," April 28, 1984, "Woodward Shootout Stirs Memories," June 18, 1984, *Centre Daily Times*, State College.

occasionally to see his family, but it was an act of defiance that could not continue without an eventual confrontation with the authorities. Ettlinger surely knew that, but his disregard for the law and his desire to see his family must have overruled his judgment on the day that word reached John Barner that the wanted man had been spotted coming into town.

There was no answer when Barner knocked at Ettlinger's locked door, so the new constable tried to break it down. He had almost succeeded when shots rang out from inside the house. The bullets hit Barner squarely in the chest, and were no doubt fatal, but the insane shooter calmly came outside and slit Barner's throat for good measure, leaving the body lying on the front porch.

Once back inside, the murderer managed to get off another shot, which wounded his neighbor, the town blacksmith, Frank Guisewhite, who had been watching the events from a window in his house across the street. Resigned to making a last stand, Ettlinger ordered his wife and two children to take the mattresses off all the beds and prop them up against the walls of the centermost room on the second floor of the house.

The thick padding kept the family safe from the fusillade that now was taking place, since by that time "scores" of angry men were in place around the Ettlinger homestead, and each one was blasting away with the rifle or shotgun they had brought with them. There were so many riflemen, and so many shots were fired, that it would later be said that when it was all over there "wasn't any ammunition to be had anywhere between Woodward and Bellefonte!" Participants and observers of the great shootout would indeed later recall that the high-powered rifle shells lying on the ground were so numerous that anybody could reach down anywhere and "pick them up by the handful."[7]

The siege continued all through the night, and at noon the next day, county sheriff John Condo, who had been summoned from Bellefonte and who was tired of the standoff, ordered the house to be torched. The fire was soon raging, and Ettlinger's wife and children managed to escape through the cellar door. With the whole house now ablaze, Ettlinger himself came out, his right arm raised over his head, and his left arm, with a .38 caliber revolver in his hand, hanging down by his side.

---

7. Ibid.

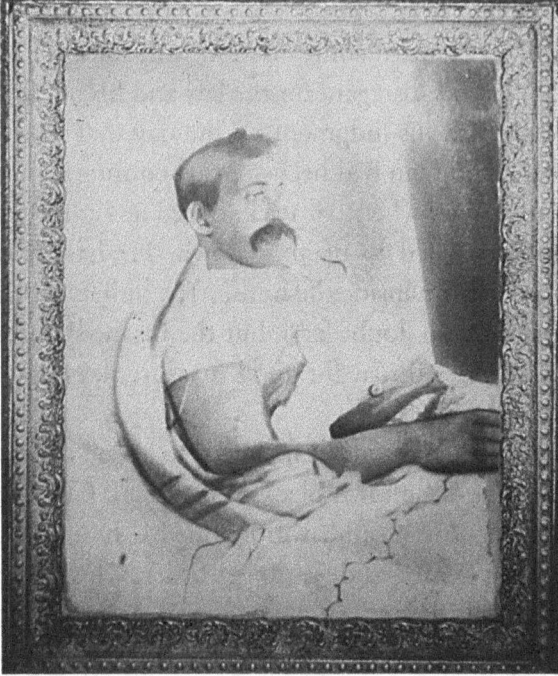

A Picture of Wounded Frank Guisewhite. This old newspaper picture of Frank Guisewhite can be found in the museum building in Aaronsburg, Centre County. Guisewhite, an innocent bystander when the big "shootout" occurred at Woodward in 1896, was shot by renegade outlaw Bill Ettlinger before authorities burned down Ettlinger's house to drive him out.

There are some who say that Ettlinger was trying to surrender, and was about to do so, until someone fired a shot. It was the final straw for the demented man, and, after shouting "Okay, if that's the way you sons a' bitches want it!" he put his gun to his head and shot himself.[8]

The "shootout at Woodward," as it would later be called, was an event that was indelibly stamped upon the minds of all those who witnessed the remarkable events. Children who were there when it all happened were especially affected. It was a terrible experience, even rivaling some of today's horrible terrorist episodes, so it is little wonder that it traumatized youngsters who saw it all take place. Not surprising, then, that the Ettlinger children, Bessie and Jay, were even more profoundly affected by the events.

8. Donald Heggenstaller (born June 19, 1936), recorded November 18, 1988.

"Do you know that Jay and his sister never got married because they wanted to shut off the Ettlinger bloodline right there?" mused Donald Heggenstaller, former editor of the Millheim Journal, during a 1988 interview. Back in the early 1950s, Heggenstaller ran a picture of Bill Ettlinger as the Guess Who photo of the week in his newspaper. Learning that Ettlinger's son resided in Johnstown, the editor called the man to tell him about it, and to see if he could get further details about the episode. "He protested and started to cry," recalled Heggenstaller. "And he said, 'Oh no, you wouldn't do that! That's not even history. Our father dishonored us!'[9]

Scarred for a lifetime, the Ettlinger children, Heggenstaller discovered, never had dated, never had married, and never had children of their own. Perhaps the events of that day, the day of the shootout at Woodward, were also so unnerving for the others who were there that subconsciously they could never get over it. Maybe that is why some claimed that every so often, on those moonless nights of the year when a cold icy wind blows down off the mountains to the north, a ghostly fire could be seen burning in Ettlinger's Woods, the forested plot where the Ettlinger home once stood before it was burned down.

But there are many who would say that the human mind can play tricks like that, can cause people to see things that aren't really there, or to interpret what they do see in an incorrect way. Logical as that idea might be, it probably would not have been an argument that would have persuaded the frightened man who entered Orndorf's store one night back in 1880, that what he had just experienced could be explained as imagination run wild.

When Mike ran into Louie Orndorf's store in Woodward that night, he was out of breath and "bawling like a baby." The brawny woodcutter had run almost all the way down into town from up on Thick Mountain, where he had been cutting timber along the little stream known locally as Oil Run. The man's emotional state and his physical condition caught Louie Orndorf and his son Ray off guard. The big lumberjack was known for bragging and always picking fights; and now here he was, not only crying like a baby but with whitened eyebrows looking like they had just been singed by fire. After he calmed down and caught his breath, Mike explained that he had worked later than usual that night, and it was almost dark when he started walking back into town. He hadn't gone far when he said he heard someone beside him say "Hi, Mike!"

---

9. Ibid.

Totally surprised by the unexpected greeting, the tough lumberman looked down and was further taken aback when he saw "this little man walking beside him." Then, to the horror of the alarmed woodsman, the midget "just disappeared in a puff of fire" that was so close and so hot that it reddened the benumbed man's face and singed his eyebrows so badly that they were almost burned off.[10]

Many years later Ray Orndorf would say that seeing this big "tough guy" in tears was a sight that struck him as somewhat comical at the time. He didn't like the man anyway, because of the way he was always bragging and "carrying on," so to see him "cut down a peg" seemed almost laughable. He had seen the distraught man's singed eyebrows, however, and they seemed to prove that something unusual must have happened to him. What that might have been, he decided, was not something he wanted to experience for himself.

Devil's fires and ghostly blazes of any kind don't seem to be something that need concern anyone today. Our modern ways of thinking have washed them from the face of the earth, or so it would seem. On the other hand, perhaps they've taken a less spectacular and more natural form. At least that might be a conclusion some could draw from an experience one woman had when she and a friend decided to visit a well-known spot on the battlefield at Gettysburg one night in 1994.

The songwriter, at the suggestion of her friend, had agreed to go to the military park to see if visiting one of its most haunted places would provide inspiration for the song she had been asked to write. She didn't want to write the piece, thinking there had already been enough said about Devil's Den, that place on the battlefield that, during the three days' engagement of July 1–3, 1863, was the sight of some of the heaviest musket firing of the entire battle.

The huge boulders of the den served as an ideal vantage point for snipers and sharpshooters, who were placed there to pick off officers of the opposing forces, and both sides held this piece of key real estate at one time or another during the bloody fighting. The site looks very much today like it did then, with the huge boulders that form the Den still sitting in the same places they sat in back in 1863.

---

10. Jean Voneida, recorded November 13, 1982.

A view of Devil's Den from Little Roundtop at Gettysburg.

Visitors today will not see brilliant bursts of cannon blasts or numerous sparkles of musket fire light up the place the way they intermittently illuminated it during the battle. On the other hand, tourists will find steps that allow them to easily walk to the top of the huge boulders, and it was very late at night, and very dark, when the songwriter and her friend climbed those same stairs.

"I felt like I was losing my balance, and then I could hear what sounded like footsteps down the hill from where I was," said the songwriter, recalling her experience that evening. "I was thinking about all the stories that had been told about this place, about the den itself, and then all of a sudden there was like a burst of fireflies that filled the night with light! Then the name William Langley just popped into my head!"

William Langley was a Confederate infantryman at the battle of Gettysburg. A member of Robertson's Brigade, 1st Texas Infantry, Hood's Division, the young southerner would have no doubt gone down in history as just another battlefield casualty had his spirit been able to find peace in death. However, there are those that say it is his ghostly apparition

Some of the large boulders that form Devil's Den at Gettysburg. They provided shelter for the Confederate sharpshooters that concealed themselves here during the three-day battle.

that sometimes appears in tourists' pictures when they take photos of the stone wall built as a protective shield by Confederate sharpshooters at the top of Devil's Den on the night of July second, 1863. And it was here, at this same stone wall on top of Devil's Den, that photographer Alexander Gardner took one of his most famous photographs, several days after the battle was over.

Anyone who has ever read anything about the fighting around Devil's Den during those terrible three days in July 1863, has probably seen Gardner's photo, which he titled "a sharpshooter's last sleep." The picture shows a dead Confederate soldier lying on his back next to the stone wall which spans the opening between two huge boulders at the top of Devil's Den. Propped against the wall and pointing to the sky is what appears to be the soldier's musket. It is a poignant photo, contrasting the youthful appearance of the dead man amidst the evident horrors of the battle, but some claim it is not an authentic scene depicting things the way Gardner found them.

Experts who have studied photos of the battle and its combatants claim that professional photographer Gardner took as many pictures of battlefield casualties as he could, since those were the scenes that would generate the highest sales of his pictures. However, by the time he got to Devil's Den, burial brigades of Union soldiers had buried most of the battle's dead combatants, and Gardner was disappointed. He had wanted to include at least one dead soldier in his pictures of the notorious Devil's Den, and now he would have to find a cadaver somewhere else. After some searching, he found the body of a Rebel soldier lying not over forty yards away, and it was this body, so claim those who have investigated the matter, that Gardner dragged to the Den and positioned among the rocks to appear as though the dead Confederate had fallen there.

Whether the photographer removed all means of identification when he moved him, or whether someone else did at another time, the dead soldier could not be identified before he was buried. No doubt he would have remained just another dead "unknown soldier" of Gettysburg had not a sharp-eyed battlefield guide taken a closer look one day at the collection of old Civil War photos stored at the Gettysburg battlefield museum. When comparing the photo of the dead Devil's Den soldier in Gardner's photo to a photo of William Langley that was taken shortly after he had enlisted into the Rebel army, the guide was immediately convinced the two men were the same.

There are those who are not so sure that a positive identification has been established, and it is Langley's spirit, so believes the songwriter who was overcome by the firefly display on the night she visited Devil's Den, that still haunts this place. He has not yet found peace, she believes, because even though he fought nobly for a cause in which he believed, and for a Confederate state that he loved, he has never been given due credit for doing so. Now his only recourse for reminding people of that fact, she says, may be resorting to supernatural means, sometimes appearing as a ghostly image in a photograph or as a modern-day version of the old ghost fires—a swarm of fireflies.[11]

---

11. Diane Smith, recorded January 25, 1998.

CHAPTER 13

CORNPLANTER TALES

Although memories of Pennsylvania's storied frontier days seem only to be kept alive in the pages of history books, there is a little-known remnant of those times that can be found yet today at the head waters of the Allegheny River in Salamanca, New York. Here, about five miles north of Pennsylvania's Allegheny National Forest lands, are the homes of some of the last surviving members of the Iroquois Nation. Among those who live here are members of the Senecas and Tuscaroras, and other tribes that once comprised the Six Nations Confederacy, that once-powerful alliance of tribes that figured so prominently in Pennsylvania's Indian wars.

Living today, on Salamanca's Allegheny Indian Reservation, are descendants of great Seneca war chiefs and leaders like Red Jacket, Handsome Lake, Governor Blacksnake, and the Cornplanter, and of others who once fought settlers for prime hunting and farming lands that the Indians considered to be rightfully theirs, but which frontiersmen coveted as their own.

It was a conflict of interest that would ultimately lead to the downfall of the Indian's way of life and to his displacement from the lands he had lived upon for so long. However, that conflict, and the displacement of tribes that often occurred because of it, continued well into the twentieth century, eventually impacting residents of Pennsylvania's own reservation in an unjust and unexpected way.

The *O-He-Yoh-Noh*, or "people of the Allegheny," as the Iroquois like to refer to themselves, offered the Pennsylvania Senecas a home when the waters of the Allegheny River flooded Pennsylvania's Cornplanter Grant in 1964. Knowing that these floodwaters would never recede, the Pennsylvania Senecas had no choice but to accept the offer from their New York kinsmen.

The flooding was, after all, not caused by a natural disaster, but by the great walls of the Kinzua Dam, built by the Army Corps of Engineers as part of a flood control project. It was just another bitter pill to swallow for the Indians who thought their Pennsylvania territory was inviolate; theirs, in the words of the original grant, for "as long as the sun shines, the grass grows green, and the water runs downhill."[1]

Despite protracted legal battles, the Cornplanter Indians lost their battle to remain on the 734 acres of land that were given to their great chieftain by Pennsylvania's provincial government in 1791, in appreciation for his support following the Revolutionary War. For almost 175 years the descendants of the great Cornplanter had lived with the thought that the words of the grant that gave them their land would be honored forever, but then in 1964 the sacred promises of the colonial authorities dissolved in the murky waters of the Allegheny, just as though they had been nothing but spun sugar. It was not an eviction that was easy to forget, and even ten years later there were many former Cornplanter Indians who longed for their original home, but they had to be content with just the memories of the place, and telling interested people its stories.

There were once many interesting accounts about the Cornplanter Grant that could be related by its former residents, but today that's probably no longer the case. However, some years ago several of us listened with rapt attention as an older Seneca woman, who was a former resident of the Cornplanter Grant, and a direct descendant of the great chief, told us some of the legends about her ancestor and her ancestral home. "The whites didn't do right by us when they built the Kinzua Dam," lamented the wizened Seneca. "My father told the government it was a bad spot for a dam. He told them it wasn't solid; that the rock would let the water leak through! Now they're finding out that was true! But we knew it was no use to argue and that we had to dig up all the graves in the old Indian burial

_____

1. Nellie Jack, interviewed August 29, 1974.

ground in order to save them from flooding, even though the Indian has always believed that the dead say 'Do not disturb me!'"[2]

It was a belief that seemed to hold some truth, according to our storyteller. At least it seemed to her that the disturbance of the many graves in the old Indian resting-place led to unquiet spirits, which manifested themselves in the form of eerie and unsettling occurrences. It was, in fact, shortly after they began digging up graves in the ancestral burial ground that the Cornplanter Indians began to hear strange sounds coming from the cemetery late at night. "One night I heard the sounds of drums coming from there, and so I went to see," recalled our storyteller. "As I got closer, I heard a song I'd never heard before. Another night I heard the sounds again, and when I got there this time, I heard a woman's voice singing a sad-sounding song somewhere in the cemetery! Not long after this we heard a scream coming from the old burial place. When the men went to look, they saw this tall white form on top of the Cornplanter Monument (the marker that was erected to immortalize the memory of the old chief)! After that we were all afraid to go into the cemetery again, and so everyone knew we had to do something to quiet the spirits."[3]

It was at this point that the Cornplanter Indians decided to call in an Indian from the nearby Cattaraugus reservation. The old Indian knew many of the Iroquois' Long House ceremonies, and after he liberally sprinkled tobacco all over the cemetery and solemnly performed the proper rites, the problems were solved. After that, said our fascinating Seneca storyteller, "we had no more trouble with ghosts!"[4]

The Seneca lady did not say so, but others might think that the "tall white form" that appeared on top of the Cornplanter monument that one particular evening was the ghost of Cornplanter himself. The chief's descendant did explain, however, that Cornplanter's wish was that he be buried in an unmarked grave. It is because of that, she noted, that his final resting-place is in a spot "known only to the Indians" and safe from the cold waters of the dam.[5]

Although his final resting-place may never be revealed to outsiders, Cornplanter's spirit will live on through the many "pen pictures" that

2. Ibid.
3. Ibid.
4. Ibid.
5. Ibid.

preserve the memory of the great chieftain and give us some idea of what he was really like. "Distinguished for talent, courage, eloquence, sobriety, and love for tribe and race, to whose welfare he devoted his time, his energy, and his means during a long and eventful life," is the way those memories were summarized on the inscription that was placed upon the monument erected to him at the Cornplanter Grant in 1866 by the state of Pennsylvania.[6]

However, words about the man known to the Indians as *Gy-ant-wa-chia* don't really capture his likeness; don't reveal the traits that might be observed if we could meet him face-to-face. "A picture is worth a thousand words," as the old saying goes, and so this holds true for Cornplanter as well.

The earliest known likeness of Cornplanter is the portrait drawn by artist F. Bartoli that hangs today on a wall of the New York Historical Society. Painted in 1796, the picture shows a relatively young man wearing a plumed helmet and in full Indian dress. In his hand he holds a smoking peace pipe decorated with assorted feathers, while dangling down from his left ear there is a loop of skin which appears to be the healed remains of a badly torn ear lobe. The portrait is obviously of a Cornplanter in his prime, but in a later drawing of the chief, showing him in the same pose and in the same outfit, he shows the effects of the passing years, having grown more wrinkled and fatter as time passed by.

There may have been numerous scars on his body as a result of the many battles in which he once took part, but other than the torn ear lobe, there are no other evident marks shown on either of his portraits that would indicate the man had been wounded in any way. To the contrary, the torn ear lobe is said to have been the result of a Philadelphia carriage accident rather than a deformity caused by some horrible wound inflicted upon him in hand-to-hand combat with a foe. But Cornplanter's descendants say he did have one such deformity; the result of a blow from an adversary that was not struck in a time of war, but rather in a time of peace.

In 1834, about a year and a half before he died, at or several years past the century mark, Cornplanter agreed to be interviewed by a young journalist who wanted to write an article about him. Although scenes of the Revolution painted by the old warrior, including its battles and the

6. C. Hale Sipe, *The Indian Chiefs of Pennsylvania*, 471–472.

generals and the Indians who fought them, left a vivid impression upon the mind of the journalist, he was equally intrigued by how "time and hardship had made dreadful impressions" upon the old man's body. "The chest was sunken, and his shoulders were drawn forward, making the upper part of his body resemble a trough," wrote the journalist. "His feet, too, were deformed and haggard by injury," noted the writer, who went on to say that he also was struck by the fact that "most of the fingers on one hand were useless," concluding that the handicap was the result of "the sinews having been severed by a blow of the tomahawk or scalping knife."[7]

The reporter's conclusions were not true, say the Senecas. They recall a different reason for the old warrior's useless hand. They say it was inflicted upon him during a peace conference. According to the Seneca account, Cornplanter's calm demeanor and firm insistence upon peaceful methods for resolving conflicts tried the patience of one of the colonists who was sitting beside him. In a fit of anger, the man smashed the peaceful Indian's hand with a heavy object, shouting "Peace, peace, all you want is peace!"[8] It was a blow strong enough to cripple the hand of the great chief, but it was not strong enough to make him abandon the lofty ideals he held for his people.

One of the things the former warrior became convinced of in his later years, as he learned more of the white man's ways, was the value of an education for the Indian. It was that conviction that finally led Cornplanter to invite the Quakers to come to his reservation in 1798 to set up a school and a mission for his people. The benevolent people of the plain sect set up their school, and many young Senecas benefited from it, but legend states that at least one non-Indian got an education there as well.

Although it's not known for sure when he attended, there was at one time a Frenchman sitting in the classroom of the Cornplanter School. Known to history as Henri Chevalier, his other claim to fame is that he had been a Napoleonic soldier and the only man to have fought under the infamous Bonaparte (at Leipsig in 1813) and against him (at Waterloo in 1815).

What brought him to this country is not remembered anymore, but history also states that he was born in Switzerland in 1800, and that when he got to America he eventually settled in Ceres, McKean County. It was

7. J. E. Henretta, *Kane and the Upper Allegheny*, 266–267.
8. Nellie Jack, interviewed August 29, 1974.

Chief Cornplanter. Painted by an unknown artist, this portrait of the great Seneca war chief was done many years after he was in his prime and an inveterate foe of the white man. For almost two-hundred years the old chief's descendants lived on the "grant" given to him by grateful Colonial authorities. The Cornplanter Grant in Warren County was Pennsylvania's only Indian reservation until it was flooded by the waters of Kinzua Dam in 1964. (Photo courtesy of Pennsylvania Historical and Museum Commission, Division of Archives and Manuscripts (RG-31, Department of Commerce.

not an easy thing to do, since he could speak no English, but eventually someone got the teacher at the Cornplanter School to agree that she would teach him the language.

The first teacher at the new Quaker school was Miss Julia L. Tomes, and perhaps it was she that took on the task of teaching the rugged soldier some English. She was resoundingly successful, so says this Cornplanter tale, because her pupil, when he had mastered the new tongue sufficiently, asked her to marry him. His command of the language must have been adequate, for his proposal was accepted, and, according to this delightful little vignette, the two "lived happily ever after."[9]

9. Frances X. Sculley, letter to the author, December 18, 1979.

Whether or not it was Miss Tomes who married Chevalier could no doubt be verified if enough research were done to clarify the matter. On the other hand, it may have been another teacher who ended up as Chevalier's bride, her name washed away in the seas of time, much like the waters of the Allegheny River have washed away other memories of the old Cornplanter Grant.

NOTE: If indeed the name of Henri Chevalier's wife has been forgotten over the years, it's surprising that his name hasn't met the same fate. At least that's the conclusion that might be reached, when the story of another Napoleonic soldier who migrated to Pennsylvania is considered.

Up in Venango County there is a tradition recalling how another old veteran of Napoleon's campaigns got off the stage one day in the town of Franklin. He rented a room in the hotel owned at that time by George Powers, and, preferring a quiet and solitary life, never made an effort to cultivate friends. Then one day he was found dead in his room. So complete had been his isolation that no one knew his name; only that he had fought under the infamous Bonaparte. They buried him in a nameless grave in the Franklin Pioneer Cemetery, and here the tomb of this unknown Napoleonic soldier can be found yet today.[10]

---

10. George Swetnam and Helene Smith, *Guidebook to Historic Western Pennsylvania*, 200.

CHAPTER 14

AN ANGRY GHOST

Angry ghosts, it is said, are not uncommon inhabitants of graveyards, and any ghost-hunting group seems to have its own favorite cemetery where they like to search for evidence of these unhappy and restless spirits. There are many such places, and over in Butler County there is probably none better known than a secluded boneyard tucked away in the wilds of Moraine State Park.

Located at the end of Burton Road on the Northeastern point of the park property, the old family plot is not shown on the park map, probably because they want to discourage the crowds that might be drawn there if the general public knew about its location and eerie reputation.

Enclosed by a wall of field stones that were cut to shape and laid up by local masons, the resting place is home to 20 gravestones, but of the 20 markers, there is one that stands out above the rest, and that is the one erected over the grave of Conrad Snyder. Snyder's stone is the largest in the cemetery and it's his that has been the focus of the lurid tales that cling to this spot.

The death date on Conrad Snyder's stone indicates he died in 1866, shortly after the end of the Civil War. It's not known whether that great conflict may have caused his spirit to be restless in some way, or whether it may have been his desire to protect the graves of his descendants for eternity, but his spirit is said to haunt this God's half-acre during the darkest nights of the year, and there are many who claim to have seen an ethereal green glow emanating from his tombstone at such times.

Others have sworn that they've been frightened away by white lights strobing from the dark shadows of the surrounding forest, and by glowing red eyes that resemble those of Satan's hellhounds. Those courageous enough to snap some pictures have subsequently found that those photos often display those strange balls of light known to ghost hunters as "orbs," and claimed by them to be evidence of ghostly presences.

Snyder Cemetery is well known to ghost hunting groups and to students at nearby Slippery Rock University, and one of those students and her friends can vouchsafe as to the strange things that happen sometimes when visitors pay a nighttime visit to this uninviting place. The three young scholars, on the spur of the moment, decided to drive up to Snyder Cemetery late one Friday night in early fall.

Once they got there and the driver parked his truck, they realized it was getting dark and they only had some cigarette lighters and a scented candle to provide light for their strange soiree. Nevertheless, they forged ahead and after passing through the ornate wrought iron gate entrance to the unnatural spot they began to investigate.

It wasn't long, according to the young lady, until they heard moaning sounds coming from the woods, and then she realized how dark it had become. The combination of sounds, darkness, and lichen-covered tombstones on all sides, soon became too much for all of them to bear and the frightened explorers ran back to the pickup truck that had brought them there. After all of them had squeezed back in the vehicle, the driver frantically kept trying to start the fairly new GMC truck, but it took five tries before the engine finally turned over.

He then lost no time in speeding away after turning on his headlights, but much to everyone's consternation the headlights kept switching back and forth between high and low beams, as though they had a mind of their own. This weird phenomenon prompted the driver to increase his speed, and the truck's occupants were roughly jostled around as the vehicle bounced down the gravel road. Then suddenly, as though it had been conjured up by evil forces to block their race to safety, a dense white cloud descended upon the truck.

The fog was so thick that the fleeing ghost hunters could not see more than several inches past the front of the truck and the driver could only

The Old Stone House at it looks today (Butler County). Currently leased from the Pennsylvania Historical Museum Commission and administered by Slippery Rock University.

discern the faint outlines of the dirt road ahead. For two miles they endured the dense fog and the erratic headlights, but when they finally exited the road, they noted that things immediately returned to normal, with dissipation of the fog and an end to the headlights' strange performance.

They encountered no other foggy areas on their way home that night, nor did the owner of the truck ever have problems with his headlights behaving in a similar erratic fashion ever again. But since that time, others have made nocturnal visits to this same cemetery, and without fail all have reported experiencing strange occurrences, ranging from sudden loss of cell phone service to strange sounds that sound like someone walking in the nearby woods and the faint echoes of Indian drums.

Not that there are any Indians buried here, but four miles to the northeast, and near a local historic landmark, there is an unmarked gravesite that holds the earthly remains of one infamous criminal who once terrorized the early settlers of the region and whose spirit is said to haunt the nearby stone house, and may, it could be surmised, also account for the sounds of those Indian drums.

Known today as the Old Stone House, the current structure is a restored version of the original building, which was erected in 1822 by businessman John Brown, who realized there was a profitable opportunity here after the recent completion of the Pittsburgh to Erie Turnpike. Even though the first permanent settler had entered this area just 26 years earlier, Brown knew that the opening of the turnpike would mean heavy wagon and stagecoach traffic moving north from the forks of the Ohio River in the south. Accordingly, he built the sturdy sandstone house to serve as an inn and a tavern at the halfway point of the 36-hour turnpike trip between Pittsburgh and Erie, and his business did indeed attract many customers—travelers and locals as well.

Customers could enjoy the hearty food served in the dining room on the first floor, and then relax in the comfort of the parlor where they could pick up news from travelers coming from distant parts of the state. Those spending the night would climb the stairs to the second floor where there was one large sleeping room partitioned by curtains and having down-filled coverlets on the floor to serve as guests' "beds."

Despite being glad for the soft beds, the weary travelers knew they had to follow the innkeeper's strict rules if they were going to stay here again, and so they removed their boots and checked to be sure they weren't exceeding the capacities outlined by the bold lettering on the weather-beaten sign at the front of the inn: "No more than five to sleep in a bed." Even then, the overnight guests were not guaranteed a good night's sleep, since not only were the sleeping quarters primitive, but the tavern room just below them was often filled with loud conversation and raucous laughter well into the wee hours of the morning.

With its rowdy and boisterous customers, many of whom were tobacco chewers spitting on the floor, the old hostelry would not have been rated as a luxury hotel by today's standards, but tradition does declare that shortly after it opened, it was respectable enough to be visited by none other than the Marquis de Lafayette, French aristocrat and military officer who provided tactical leadership to Washington's Continental Army and who secured vital resources from France during the Revolutionary War.

In its first decades, the wayside inn also served as a post office, and then as a muster point for Civil War volunteers. Its decline began shortly after that with highwaymen, horse thieves, counterfeiters and other undesirables finding it a safe retreat where they could blend in with legitimate customers and stay out of the hands of law enforcement officials who were few and far between at that time. Then with the advent of the railroad in the 1870s, the flux of highway travelers dropped off dramatically until it was no longer profitable to keep the inn open.

A farm family moved in for a while, renting rooms for the night to an occasional traveler, but then the historic place was finally abandoned in 1918 and left to the destructive forces of the elements. There was one guest who remained there, however, or more appropriately we should say his spiritual essence lingered there, either because it had nowhere else to go or because it wanted to stay close to the nearby Venango Path; the old Indian trail that extended from the forks of the Ohio to Lake Erie in the north, much like the turnpike that was opened in 1822. On the other hand, the fixated ghost may have stubbornly refused to leave, mooring itself there out of spite.

The spiteful reason the grounded phantom may still haunt the old inn is a sad one, beginning with events that historians referred to as the last Indian massacre in Pennsylvania. This horrific episode occurred on July first, 1843, in Slippery Rock Township, almost within a stone's throw of the Old Stone House Inn. The result of this bloody crime was that it created a decades-long animosity toward any Indians who subsequently passed through the area, and it may also have led to the vengeful poltergeist which now haunts the inn.

In those days it was not unusual for Native Americans from New York state reservations on the Upper Allegheny to serve as raftsmen of log rafts, steering them down the Allegheny River to lumber buyers in Pittsburgh and then returning home via stagecoach on the Pittsburgh-Erie Pike. With Butler at the halfway point on the turnpike, the returning raft pilots would often spend the night there, with usually no incidents of lawlessness. That changed on June 29, 1843, when residents in the area spotted a drunken and pugnacious Indian raft pilot accosting people in threatening ways and having violent outbursts.

Subsequent inquiries revealed that the Indian, whose name was Sam Mohawk, was a well-known terror in the region whenever he came down

Sam Mowhawk (artist's rendition). (Drawing by Steven Collins. Used with the artist's permission and courtesy of Butler County Historical Society.)

from the Seneca Indian reservation in Cattaraugus County, New York. He had a foul reputation as a mean drunk once intoxicated, and also tended to be nasty with women. On this particular day, it seemed he was exhibiting those qualities in excess, in part because he had been fighting with his wife before boarding his raft and heading down the river. Locals reported that on this occasion he was "just going crazy."

Mohawk spent that night in Butler but left in an angry huff the next day when all the bars in town refused to serve him whisky. He then rode a stage to the Stone House Tavern where he took offense when proprietor John Sill refused to serve him any more liquor as well. A fight ensued and Sill threw the drunken man out of the tavern, after breaking a chair over his head to ensure compliance.

The Indian had no place to go, and spent that night sleeping on the ground outside the tavern, which no doubt contributed to his foul mood when he awoke the morning of July first. Dazed and maddened by alcohol withdrawal symptoms, Mohawk stumbled off, eventually arriving at the log home of James Wigton.

A light in an outbuilding alerted Mohawk that somebody might be inside, and when he entered the weathered structure, he found Wigton's wife Margaret, age 29, in the smokehouse cutting meat. The pioneer lady was taken by surprise and was immediately alarmed by Mohawk's threatening manner. A bolt of fear must have shot through her at that instant also, when she recalled she was alone, her husband having gone off that morning to his father's house a few miles distant to buy a horse. Knowing it was either flight or fight, she picked up a knife to defend herself, and to protect her children that were inside their log home.

Maddened by the woman's defensive stance, the enraged Indian grabbed the defiant woman, and in the ensuing struggle Mrs. Wigton held her own for a while, even managing to inflict a deep gash on the Indian's head with her knife. But the brute strength of the attacker finally prevailed, after he picked up a heavy stick and hit the feisty lady over the head. Thinking he had killed her, he then went to the Wigton homestead where he found the Wigton children: Elmira, 7; Jeninah Nancy, 6; Perry, 4; Amanda, 2; and John Wallace, the youngest, about 9 months old, sleeping inside.

However, Mrs. Wigton, revived and spurred on by her strong motherly instincts, still had enough life left in her to get up and run to her offspring. Here she managed to force herself through the cabin's door despite Mohawk's attempts to hold it shut, but once she was inside, she was once again set upon by Mohawk, who had by this time picked up a large stone lying near the fireplace.

Driven by his fury and his alcoholic delirium, the crazed Indian coldly used the rock to beat out Mrs. Wigton's brains. Then in a murderous rampage he mercilessly did the same to the young son who was asleep in a cradle in the kitchen and to all four of her sleeping children upstairs.

Sam Mohawk fled from the house after completing his massacre, leaving six bloody bodies behind and the walls and ceiling of the cabin splattered with blood and brains. Those surveying the horrid scene later would also find a large oblong rock covered with blood lying on the floor; the murder weapon left behind by the murderer.

This was the sight that greeted Lemuel Davis and his son and nephew when they later arrived at the Wigton farm to help them in the fields. Seeing no one about, Davis knocked on the door, and receiving no answer, walked in. He was never to forget the sight, and soon people from far and wide had heard the news and had gathered at the Wigton homestead. It was this crowd of people that greeted James Wigton when he came back home.

He was informed of the fate of his family and Wigton stood motionless until he recovered from his shock. It was minutes before he could finally speak, and then he insisted upon seeing his wife and children. Those present would not allow it, but instead insisted he go with them to track down the murderer, who by this time had been identified by those who saw him fleeing the scene.

The would-be posse shortly became aware that the culprit had gone to the home of Philip Kiester, where the old veteran of the War of 1812 and his sons had managed to trap him inside the house. Mills, mines, and schools closed down as the word of the massacre spread, and soon a large crowd of angry men converged on the Kiester place. Despite their numbers it was with some difficulty that the vigilantes were finally able to subdue the fugitive. In the process of doing so, their level of anger had been driven to such a fever pitch that they decided that they would now either shoot him down like a dog or hang him on the spot.

However, at the insistence of Reverend Stewart and of Sheriff James Campbell and other law enforcement officials, the rush to justice was quelled and the crowd reluctantly melted away after those in authority insisted that they should let the law take its course. The prisoner was then tightly bound and placed in Jesse Kiester's wagon. Along with an armed guard of 25 men, he was roughly transported to the Wigton homestead to attend an inquest and then off to the jail in Butler to await trial.

Once at the jail he was taken to a cell resembling a dungeon and there he was chained to an iron ring in the floor and kept that way until he was brought to trial the following December. After four days of testimony by 48 witnesses, it took the jury less than an hour to find the defendant guilty. He was sentenced to death with his hanging to take place on March 22, 1844. It was to be the first criminal execution in the county.

On that day the streets of Butler were crowded with those hoping to view the hanging. Most were disappointed, since it could only be seen by those perched on top of the walls surrounding the jail yard. Afterwards the deceased man's body was placed in a wooden coffin and loaded on another wagon, which, when about a mile out of town, rolled into a corner of a field on the McCall farm where an internment was conducted.

To this day the exact site of the grave is unknown. However, Margaret Wigton and all five of her children were already resting peacefully in a common grave in the Muddy Creek Cemetery, Clay Township, where a large marble tombstone bearing their names marks their resting place today.

Although the Wigtons seem to have found peace in the next world there are those who think that Sam Mohawk did not. This is particularly true of those who serve as guides and docents at the Old Stone House, for it is here that the ghost of Sam Mohawk seems to be most active.

Those working there have reported, and still experience, many unexplainable events. Some say they've seen ghostly visions in the house, while others claim to have heard maniacal laughter coming from downstairs, and have seen candles flame up on their own upstairs but then go out when someone investigates.

Those of a more practical and logical turn of mind reason that these phenomena are easily explained by some natural cause; and the whole idea of the old wayside inn being haunted arose, in the first place, from the fact that the criminals who once used the out-of-the-way tavern for their nefarious purposes, made up the stories of hauntings to keep from being discovered, to keep people away.

The Old Stone House employees who have experienced at least one seemingly supernatural event at the old inn would take exception to such claims. On some evenings in mid-summer when they are locking the place down for the night, they are sometimes jarred by a loud noise coming from the second floor. It sounds to them just like someone standing up there has just dropped or thrown a large stone down on the floor in a fit of anger!

NOTE: Details for this story were obtained from the book titled *Rage, Murder, and Execution! The Story of Sam Mohawk and the Wigton Family Massacre,* by Bradley Pflugh, and from conversations with employees at the Old Stone House during my visit there on September 9, 2012.

ACKNOWLEDGMENTS

To all those who love the Pennsylvania mountains and the legends and folktales that have grown up around them. May you enjoy the stories as much as I've enjoyed collecting and writing about them.

BIBLIOGRAPHY

Aldrich, Lewis Cass, *History of Clearfield County, Pennsylvania*, Syracuse, NY, D. Mason and Company, 1887.

Anderson, Barbara M., editor, *Haines Township Life and Tradition*, Haines Township Bicentennial Book Committee, Aaronsburg, PA, 1976.

Bartlett, John, *Familiar Quotations*, Boston, Little, Brown, & Company, 2019.

Beers, J. H. & Co., *History of the Counties of McKean, Elk, and Forest, Pennsylvania*, Chicago, 1890.

Blackman, Emily C., *History of Susquehanna County, Pennsylvania*, Philadelphia, Claxton, Remsen & Haffelfinger, 1873.

Blunt, Arden M., editor, *Gregg Township Bicentennial, Two Hundred Years Remembered*, Gregg Township Civic Action Committee, Spring Mills, PA, 1977.

Brendle, Thomas R., and William S. Troxell, "Pennsylvania German Folk Tales, Legends, Once-a-upon-a-time Stories, Maxims, and Sayings," *Proceedings of the Pennsylvania German Society, Volume L*, Norristown, PA, Pennsylvania German Society, 1944.

Bronner, Simon J., *Popularizing Pennsylvania*, University Park, PA, The Penn State University Press, 1996.

Coco, Gregory, *On the Bloodstained Field*, Gettysburg, PA, Thomas Publications, 1987.

Day, Sherman, *Historical Collections of the State of Pennsylvania*, Port Washington, NY, Ira J. Friedman, 1843.

Faris, John T., *Old Trails and Roads in Penn's Land*, Philadelphia, J. B. Lippincott Company, 1927.

Fletcher, Stevenson W., *Pennsylvania Agriculture & Country Life, 1640–1840*, Harrisburg, PA, Pennsylvania Historical and Museum Commission, 1971.

Furnas, J. C., *The Americans, A Social History of the United States 1587–1914*, New York, G. P. Putnam's Sons, 1969.

Godcharles, Frederic A., *Daily Stories of Pennsylvania*, Milton, PA, The Hammond Press, 1924.

Grimm, Herbert L., and Paul L. Roy, *Human Interest Stories of the Three Days' Battles at Gettysburg*, Gettysburg, PA, Times and News Publishing Co., 1927.

Hain, H. H., *History of Perry County, Pennsylvania,* Harrisburg, PA, Hain-Moore Co., 1922.

Hardwick, Charles, *Traditions, Superstitions, and Folk-lore, (Chiefly Lancashire and the North of England),* Manchester, England, A. Ireland & Co., 1872.

Heckewelder, Reverend John, *History, Manner, and Customs of the Indian Nations,* Philadelphia, Lippincott's Press, 1876.

Henretta, J. E., *Kane and the Upper Allegheny,* Philadelphia, The John C. Winston Company, 1929.

Hollister, H., *History of the Lackawanna Valley,* Scranton, PA, M. Norton, bookseller and stationer, 3rd edition, 1875.

Ingram, John H., *The Haunted Homes and Family Traditions of Great Britain,* London, Reeves and Turner, 1905.

Jones, Uriah J., *History of the Early Settlement of the Juniata Valley,* Harrisburg, PA, Telegraph Press, 1889.

Kootz, Wolfgang, *Rhine Guide from Mainz to Cologne,* Kuntzverlag Edm. Von Konig, 1998.

Korson, George, *Pennsylvania Songs and Legends,* Baltimore, Johns Hopkins Press, 1949.

Linn, John Blair, *History of Centre and Clinton Counties, Pennsylvania,* Philadelphia, Louis H Everts Co., 1883.

McKnight, William J., *Pioneer Outline History of Northwestern Pennsylvania,* Philadelphia, J. B. Lippincott Co., 1905.

Meginness, John F., *Otzinachson, A History of the West Branch Valley,* Williamsport, PA, Gazette Printing House, 1889.

Mitchell, Edwin V., *It's an Old Pennsylvania Custom,* New York, NY, Vanguard Press, Inc., 1947.

Pflugh, Bradley, *Rage, Murder, and Execution! The Story of Sam Mohawk and the Wigton Family Massacre,* Butler, PA, Butler County Historical Society, 2011.

Potter County Historical Society authors, *Historical Sketches of Potter County,* Coudersport, PA, published by the society, 1976.

Rhoads, Samuel N., *Mammals of Pennsylvania and New Jersey,* Lancaster, PA, Wickersham Printing Co., 1903.

Sassaman, Grant N., editor, *Pennsylvania A Guide to the Keystone State,* Pennsylvania Writers' Project, New York, Oxford University Press, 1940.

Sipe, C. Hale, *The Indian Chiefs of Pennsylvania,* Butler, PA, Ziegler Printing Co., 1927.

Stoddard, John L., *John L. Stoddard's Lectures, Volume VIII – The Rhine,* Boston, Balch Brothers Co., 1898.

Swetnam, George, and Smith, Helene, *A Guidebook to Historic Western Pennsylvania,* Pittsburgh, PA, University of Pittsburgh Press, 1976.

Tome, Phillip, *Pioneer Life; or, Thirty Years a Hunter,* Baltimore, Gateway Press, 1989, reprint of the 1854 edition.

ABOUT THE AUTHOR

JEFFREY R. FRAZIER was born and raised in Centre Hall, Centre County, where he says he grew up in a "Tom Sawyer sort of way," later graduating with a BS from Penn State in 1967, and then an MBA from Rider University in New Jersey in 1978. Some of the fondest memories of his boyhood include explorations of out-of-the-way spots in the mountains and hearing accounts of the legends that seem to cling to them. Then, beginning in 1970, he began collecting those same kind of anecdotes from all over the state; ranging from the Blue Mountains of Berks and Lehigh Counties, the South Mountains of Adams County, the "Black Forest" area of Potter and Tioga Counties, the Alleghenies of Clearfield and Blair Counties, and the other counties in the middle. He has compiled his vast collection of tales into an eight-volume series titled *Pennsylvania Fireside Tales*. This volume is a continuation of his work, written in a format that the average reader can enjoy, especially for those who love the green valleys and cloud-covered mountain peaks of Pennsylvania as much as he does.

www.ingramcontent.com/pod-product-compliance
Lightning Source LLC
Chambersburg PA
CBHW011200090426
42740CB00020B/3414